Willingly

*Take Hold of Faith's Hand,
and Experience Freedom from Fear's Grip!*

By Sherrie Brown

Praise for "Willingly"

"Sherrie Brown is a remarkable woman of God. Her confidence is in the Lord's power and love. Her book "Willingly" – filled personal testimonies along with her prayers, are being used by God to ignite faith in every person who reads them.

Sherrie takes no credit for herself – her desire is always to share with others what God has done, for Him to receive all the Glory. Her book gives its reader an invitation to walk with the Lord in a more wonderfully powerful way.

Willingly compels believers to embrace a deeper walk of faith, and trust in Jesus."

~Peggy Hurd, MS-MFT

"We met Sherrie Brown 20 years ago while pastoring in Kirkland, Washington. Sherrie has grown tremendously in her walk with the Lord, displaying her faith and love for Jesus boldly. She has exhibited great faith and courage, declaring the Word of God over every obstacle in life. Reading "Willingly" will increase your faith and trust in Jesus. Sherrie's strong faith is contagious and leads others to partake in the supernatural work of the Lord on a daily basis."

~Pastor Bob and Donitta, Victory Life Center

"Elijah was known to be a man of prayer and I believe Sherrie Brown is a modern day Elijah to our generation. Her surrendered and obedient life has opened different

doors to see the power of God in her life and the lives of many others.

Prayer, surrender and obedience is the fruit of her ministry which is evident by the encounters and stories you will read in her book, and there is a boldness in her that comes from the place of intimacy with The Lord.

Her book is a must read because it points out the importance of a surrendered life and her stories are an extension of walking with Jesus Christ. I have witnessed her powerful prayers for me and others.

This book will align you to live a life of surrender, intimacy and obedience which are important keys to the great move of God that is coming upon us."

~Pastor Folake Kellogg, The Collective Church

Another well done work by Sherrie Brown. Through her captivating writings, Sherrie invites us into her encounters with God. She illustrates what walking with God looks like in real time with profound life lessons that all are sure to learn from. With a knack for using humor and humility, she captures the very real struggles and learnings that life has to offer. She is real and transparent about her experiences, allowing the reader to intimately see her process. Her writing is illustrative and inviting, inviting the reader to walk more closely with the Lord on a daily basis.

~Lisa Sullivan, M.A., Psy.D, LMHC, A Sign of Hope, LLC

"When the road seems dark,
and the future looks dim,
You broaden our path with Your light
and love; laying out a red carpet
of Your grace and favor."

I dedicate my book 'Willingly' to my Savior, Deliverer, Redeemer, Restorer, and Provider, Jesus.

Also, I give thanks to my husband Steve who has been my shoulder to lean on and help mate through the years.

And lastly I thank my past, even though it was difficult at the time, I discovered much about the Nature and true Character of my Loving and Gracious Father Jesus.

Table of Contents

Introduction

We yield to You Lord, encountering You as we learn to step into a life of faith and not waver through unbelief.

The promises for our future, to which You call us, existed before we did. May we not be blinded by the size of our trials but keep our eyes on You. We will heed Your instructions and remove our hands from the steering wheel of life – willing to take the back seat and trust You as our Driver."

This has been our prayer throughout our marriage. We want all that God has for us, and we let Him know we are "ALL IN!"

After seeing we had missed the mark too many times, not allowing Jesus complete access to our lives, we sat and let the Lord know our regret. We had not been fully persuaded God knew precisely what He was doing; therefore, we took every opportunity to make our own plans and used His as backup plans.

We felt the anointing break off the yoke of fear when spending time with Jesus and sincerely repenting.

Waving our white flags of surrender, we switched gears from fear to faith and also the direction our lives were headed.

My book, Willingly, is packed full of miracles, signs, and wonders, we experienced and our testimonies of God's greatness and goodness.

You will feel empowered with great faith to launch out in faith, upon waters that may look tumultuous and deep, but God's Grace and Favor lay waiting.

My hope is for all of God's children to experience the nature of Jesus. I wholeheartedly believe that when we entirely release our lives to God, we will discover the depth of His loving-kindness and exceeding goodness.

Jesus said, "Come away with me."

I went

"Willingly"

Book 1

by Sherrie Brown

Chapter 1

When Jesus Called,
I Went Willingly

Jesus called me into His loving arms 34 years ago. I quickly turned from the direction I was headed, leaving behind a life of poor decisions and their consequences, which had led to my miserable lifestyle.

Throughout the years, before yielding to the Lord's invitation, I endured suffering and devastation, which – quite literally – ravaged my life.

From the time I was a young child and into my teens, my home was extremely volatile. At the age of five, I heard the screams of my mom as my dad beat her, and at the age of 16, CPS took me out of my home because he was doing the same thing to me.

No foundation of love had been established in my family – only the groundwork of fear was laid.

Before Jesus, I was near a nervous breakdown, having to wrestle with fear and anxiety for years. While growing up, I was told I would never accomplish a thing because I was stupid, a loser and a quitter. My family would hurl insults at me, time and time again. Living for years with physical, verbal, and emotional abuse created enormous pain in my soul, to a depth I did not realize. This led to a life of alcohol and drugs.

After reaching a place of complete desperation, feeling divided, and in pieces, I went to church with a friend when I was 29.

It was then, I invited Jesus into my heart, and felt safe and secure for the first time in my life.

Over the years I would dream of a time when I would meet someone whose arms, I would be willing to fall into.

At the age of 29, I fell into the Arms of Jesus, and ever since, I have kept falling. He is my FIRST love and remains so.

It was then that I felt the redemptive power of God literally shift my perspective from great sorrow into God's strength and joy. It was if I were standing in sinking sand, being lowered into whatever lay beneath, and suddenly placed on a mountaintop.

Life seemed brighter, and I had clarity in my mind, along with hope, which was something I had not felt before.

He is my Bread of life, my Light, and my Doorway to freedom. Jesus is my good Shepherd, and Resurrection, my Way, Truth, and Vine, while I rest as a branch.

I pray frequently to be grounded in God's perfect love, and live in quiet trust and peace.

David said, "Oh my soul, why are you in despair?" If I want to feel God's peace and presence in my soul, I've found I must first repent for giving into fear.

Each day I begin with a keen awareness of who I am, and where my past took me. I've learned to live a lifestyle of repentance and ask for God's PERFECT LOVE to search me, convict me, cover me, and complete me.

Before I received Jesus, my friends thought I had my life together because of the success I portrayed. I owned my own business, and I was also buying my home at the age of 26. By the world's standards, I appeared to be a successful young woman, however, most folks did not see that my life was rapidly spinning out of control.

I had found ways to conceal my emotions: smiling when feeling sorrow, projecting happiness when experiencing extreme despair. The intense suffering within my soul often paralyzed me, leaving me inconsolable.

There was a room in my soul, which I would retreat to, and I'd lock myself away, enduring the pain while living a life of pretense. This room was my place to be absent, to avoid having to feel and confront the utter hopelessness in which I lived.

Today, since Jesus has taken up residence in me, the healing I'd longed for throughout my life now lives within.

Psalm 23:3-4 (NIV): "He refreshes my soul. He leads me beside quiet waters, and He refreshes my soul. He guides me along the right paths for His name's sake. Even though I walk through the darkest valley, I will fear not evil; Your rod and staff, they comfort me."

"Lord Jesus, take our lives and lead us into the land filled with Your promises. Remain at our side as we walk together, through the valleys, and up to the mountain tops.

We are reminded You'll never leave us; therefore, we'll remain confident while You take places we have yet to visit. We trust You, Lord, with our whole heart, and we are ready and willing to live in Your world, walking away from our own.

From this day forward, we will wait on You Lord, seeking Your ways, no longer our own.

We fully release our lives into Your hands, only desiring what You have for us. You are good Lord, preparing only Your best for us, making it easy to abide."

Chapter 2

I Came OUT of Darkness!

Before inviting Jesus into my heart, I did not understand yet, of all I had welcomed into my life.

It was not until later, I had an epiphany, I was in more darkness, feeling less hopeful and depressed; certainly opposite of what I was searching for.

It was in this distinct place; I dedicated my entire life to Jesus. I had heard about Jesus, read about Jesus, and knew of Him; however, it was not explained to me in a way I could conceive.

Once my spiritual eyes were opened to the truth, I was quickly drawn toward Jesus, experiencing His intentional love clutching me. I could tangibly feel Jesus pulling me to His side.

Fortunately for me, I had mentors in my life, showing me the scriptures, which led me to God's victory.

But also the words penned by My Savior let me know there would be a fierce battle as well, reminding me I already won.

Jesus continues to bring me along, line upon line, and from glory to glory. He brings me in, carries me through, and ushers me to the entrance of my heritage; which is the freedom I had been seeking.

Year after year, I am building testimonies of the thrilling adventures, with God taking me up and over, ushering me toward His many blessings.

Deuteronomy 31:8 (NIV): "The Lord Himself goes before you and will be in you; he will never leave you nor forsake you. Do not be afraid; do not be discouraged."

Lamentations 3:22-26 (NIV): "Because of the Lord's great love we are not consumed, for his compassions never fail. They are new every morning; great is Your faithfulness. I say to myself; The Lord is my portion; therefore, I will wait for Him. The Lord is good to those whose hope is in Him, to the one who seeks Him. It is good to wait quietly for the salvation of the Lord."

"Lord Jesus, we celebrate You each day, for it is You Who sustains us, and makes our feet to stand and not waver through unbelief.

We will continue to seek Your face, waiting to hear from You; therefore, our path will be protected our way made perfect.

As you lead us, we will be transformed, and as we follow, we will be made whole. Our once-terrified souls will yield to the quiet trust our souls were seeking, and the comfort they longed for.

We are in awe of You, and Your love for us, Lord. You came for us all, and we will remain steadfast in Your love." Amen.

Chapter 3

Then and Now!

As I gaze over my life with Jesus, I see a path not perfectly walked but wonderfully watched over by my heavenly Father, Who is my faithful friend.

I owned and operated a successful hair salon for over 25 years before stepping away many years ago. I volunteered and worked in public schools throughout my life. I have two Patents on leg wear, and a registered trademark for Classy Calves Leg Wear™.

I recently wrote and released my first book, "Life Within His Promises."

My biggest joy, apart from Jesus, has been my family. I have a loving, supportive husband, and a beautiful family for whom I am grateful beyond words.

Impossibilities before me continue to bow at the feet of Jesus, making inroads to the possible. I see the Lord creating tangible opportunities, opening doors, and breathing life into my dreams, offering beauty for ashes and strength for my tears.

Jesus took my lowest points and made them my highest and transformed areas of desolation into fruitful places of a grand celebration. I have determined to remain childlike in my faith, keeping my relationship with Jesus of utmost importance, daily confessing Him as my first love.

Each day, He calls me into a quiet place of trust and surrender, where I find His peace waiting.

The Lord often speaks, saying, "Sherrie, trust Me, for I Am able, and all things are possible when you believe!"

Isaiah 40:4-5 (NIV): "Every valley shall be raised up, every mountain and hill made low; rough ground shall become level, the rugged places plain. And the glory of the Lord will be revealed, and all people will see it together. For the mouth of the Lord has spoken."

Deuteronomy 6:17-25 (NIV): "Be sure to keep the commands of the Lord your God and the stipulations and decrees He has given you. Do what is right and good in the Lord's sight so it will go well with you, and you we may go in and take over the good land the Lord has promised on oath to our ancestors, thrusting out all your enemies before you, as the Lord said.

In the future, when your son asks you, "What is the meaning of the stipulations, decrees, and laws the Lord our God has commanded you?" Tell him, "We were slaves of Pharaoh in Egypt, but the Lord brought us out of Egypt with a mighty hand.

Before our eyes, the Lord sent signs and wonders – great and terrible – on Egypt and Pharaoh and his whole household. But He brought us out from there to bring us in and give us the land He promised on oath to our ancestors.

The Lord commanded us to obey all these decrees and to fear the Lord our God so that we might always prosper and be kept alive, as is the case today. And if we are careful to obey all this law before the Lord our God, as he has commanded us, that will be our righteousness."

"Lord Jesus, saying we are grateful seems small, and at times we feel there are no words to express our thankfulness for Your loving-kindness.

We yield to You each day, falling into Your arms, feeling the weight of the cares we once carried, lifted. As a branch rests in the vine, so we are grafted into You; while in a posture of dependency, relying on You for every breath we take.

May the words from our mouths and the works of our hands bring Your favor; as you smile over our lives, seeing our heart, which is positioned to do Your will."
Amen.

Chapter 4

Change in Our Direction

I t was crystal clear to my husband Steve and I; God was asking us to move further than we had ever been.

In 2008 we were leaders in our church, tithed, and gave our offerings, held Bible studies, held prayer groups in our home, and shared God's love in the workplace.

He and I felt we had achieved success in creating a secure place to exist within all areas of our lives.

We made sure our decisions would not be too risky, taking all precautions, having our ducks in a row. We typically prepared for any issues, which could arise, ensuring we had solutions in place.

In the past, our walk of faith had tangible impartations of God's favor. He rewarded our obedience and trust in Him by demonstrating His wonder-working power. However, we clearly understood He was calling us to an entirely new place in our relationship, inviting us to rest, and not strive.

One morning while reading our devotional, the author asked, "Are you on the road to something mediocre or miraculous?" We both answered mediocre.

Suddenly, as if a veil were lifted, we clearly understood we would never rise past the meager level of faith in which we had been living.

We knew God wanted to take us deeper than we have ever gone, and higher into His Kingdom realm, where His mysteries are unearthed.

After reading the compelling question in our devotional, we let the Lord know we were clay on His Potter's Wheel.

Our desire is to eagerly to submit every detail of our lives moving forward. Our prayer was, "If You want to send us somewhere, Lord, to live and work, we are willing."

We returned from our vacation and Steve returned to his workplace. He searched on his company website for job openings, looking for the Lord to lead him to a location that would need his skill set.

He found a few places throughout the nation and sent out his resume. Then we waited on the Lord.

He heard back right away. All the job offerings had closed except for one, and it was the one God had singled out for us. The Lord made it clear this was the place, and within seven weeks we had moved away from the state I had called home my entire life.

Our prayer opened the door to a five-year journey, where God instructed us how to live in His amazing grace and miracle-working power.

We both felt incredible peace, as though God had placed us in a bubble of faith and sent us on a path; descending on a long slope, rolling along effortlessly for miles.

Isaiah 6:8 (NIV): "Then I heard the voice of the Lord saying, 'Whom shall I send? And who will go for us?' And I said, 'Here am I, send me!'"

John 10:27 (NIV): "My sheep listen to my voice; I know them, and they follow Me."

"Lord Jesus, may we hear You speaking, as we sit in silent rest, waiting for Your voice. Not us, never us, Lord, only You. May we continue to see You go before us and open the door before us, like a gentleman.

We will go when You say go, and remain in place when you say stand still. We will see the exit sign, lit up, if confusion has entered into our minds when we find ourselves in a place we were not meant to be.

Thank You, Lord, for always making a way out when we find ourselves in, and for making a way in if we find ourselves out. You ARE the way, the truth, and the life!" Amen.

Chapter 5

God Anointed Our Move

Steve's company paid for all our travel, flying us in when searching for a home in a new state and back home.

Our move came with many provisions, one of which was a professional company that packed our entire household. These folks moved everything into our new place and unpacked it when we arrived at our new home, hauling away all the large and small boxes.

It was a dream come true because, in the past, when we would move, we would be utterly exhausted from all the hard work of packing, unpacking, loading a few trucks and unloading. This was a time to rest in what the Lord had provided.

During our five years away, we felt supernatural ease, as if we were cutting frozen butter with a hot knife. The Presence of God, was discernible leaving us feeling hemmed in, with a shield around us, opening all doors.

Before this particular season, we had attempted to go places when God had not said "yes" to us. In the past, no ease was felt, only closed doors, facing challenging paths that lacked our King Jesus' presence.

Little did we know we were actually living in Kairos time.

Kairos, in Ancient Greek, means "the right, critical, or opportune moment for action to be taken."

We would pray our prayer, and immediately doors would open. God answered our prayer requests in ways we had never previously experienced. There was a quickening, a divine acceleration if you will, toward every utterance we made toward our loving Father. What sometimes would take months or years happened suddenly.

Doors opened quickly, and each question we asked, in terms of our needs, was answered with a resounding "yes" from the Lord.

God would continually call us to face unfamiliar situations. We knew each time we willingly made our way toward His voice, He was stretching our tent stakes, creating more room for His Spirit within us. We felt ourselves being transformed into vessels of faith and hope.

Steve and I would look at an impossible task; however, instead of feeling defeat, we would see it as an opportunity to dig deeper into Gods Word and experience His flawless character.

Frequently placing our ear to heaven's floor, we would wait to hear His voice, eager to do what He asked.

God kept us hidden, like a mother lion keeping her cubs safe as predators lingered about. Continually throughout our journey we experienced the protection of the Lord.

Much like a baby resting in its mother's womb, requiring the umbilical cord to survive, we were taught how to be the branch resting in the vine.

Before entering into our new training ground we would pray, instead of walking in on our own, as we had done years previous.

Throughout our marriage, we would talk about the direction we wanted to go, think about it, but not pray about how the Lord wanted us to proceed. We would open closed doors, making our way forward, then finding out further down the road God had not opened the door – we had.

The Lord was teaching us to be still – keenly listening and aware of God's presence, being absolutely sure He was directing us. Fearful thoughts assaulted our minds; while we were in the school of learning how to hear God's voice better. We were able to grow in our ability to apprehend His peace and sense His nod to move forward.

The enemy of intimidation, which had tried to knock us off our path, could not crash our faith party, although it did not stop him from trying.

We were adhering to our instructions from the Lord, applying our new lessons quickly, asserting our faith while in the battles we faced.

God continued to make a way, laying low obstacles, creating ways where there were none to be seen in the natural realm.

This supernatural domain in which we found ourselves was visible. We were literally watching God's Kingdom come, and seeing His will be done on earth as it is in heaven.

Matthew 6:10 (NIV): "Your Kingdom come, Your will be done, on earth as it is in heaven."

Isaiah 64:8 (NIV): "Yet You, Lord, are our Father. We are the clay, You are the Potter; we are all the work of your hand."

Isaiah 43:19 (AMP): "Listen carefully, I am about to do a new thing, now it will spring forth; will you not be aware of it? I will even put a road in the wilderness and rivers in the desert."

2 Corinthians 10:5 (NLT): "We demolish arguments and every pretension that sets itself up against the knowledge of God, and we take captive every thought to make it obedient to Christ."

"Lord Jesus, having done all to stand, we stand and watch You move on our behalf. We long for Your Kingdom to come and be displayed in our lives, Lord. When You lead, we will follow, knowing You will fiercely guard us before and behind. We surrender to Your perfect will Lord while walking this joy-filled journey. May You find our praises toward You, create a habitation for Your dwelling." Amen.

Chapter 6

The Big Giveaway

After we earnestly prayed, asking the Lord what we should do with the home we left behind, He answered, "Let a ministry use it, and do not charge them."

Initially, we were shocked, sharing with each other how we thought it would be entirely out of the realm of possibilities. Our current rent was almost twice as much as our house payment.

Then we stopped, laughed, and said, "Oh, this MUST be God," for we would never come up with this idea, not in a million years. We knew it was God's voice we heard, for it genuinely seemed irrational in our realm, but rational in God's Kingdom realm. It's comical now, looking back over this season, encountering God when He asked us to participate with Him, moving toward what seemed illogical and irrational.

We have learned to write down the message if we believe we heard God speak when waiting for answers. Negative, fear-filled thoughts persisted in their attempts to impact our minds. The enemy of our souls was hoping to derail us from God's divine plan, but we knew we had heard correctly.

Not being swayed by the doubt, we reached out to an organization, serving missionaries who are home on leave and in great need of emotional healing and physical rest.

These folks were thrilled with our offer to allow them to use our residence as a sanctuary.

The mere thought our home would be a refreshing and renewal center warmed our hearts!

This request from the Lord, to offer our home for free, came when the United States was in the midst of a pretty substantial recession, one that went on for a few years.

Americans were losing their jobs and homes at an alarming rate, making it all the more exciting for us as we watched God meet all our needs. God kept furnishing finances every step of the way. In our spirits, we sensed this was only the tip of the iceberg concerning all that God directed us toward.

My husband and I knew the funds to accomplish what God had requested would not come from his employer; we needed supernatural provision from above. As I shared our monthly rent was almost double our house payment; therefore, we knew we must trust God at His Word, believing the funds would come when we needed them.

Steve works for an excellent company that pays him well. It was clear to us that, without God intervening, we would need even more, and each month more arrived.

Habakkuk 2:2 (NIV): "Then the LORD said to me, 'Write my vision plainly on tablets, so that a runner can carry the correct message to others.'"

Luke 6:38 (NIV): "Give and it will be given to you. A good measure, pressed down, shaken together and running over, will be poured into your lap. For with the measure you use, it will be measured to you."

Ephesians 3:20 (NIV): "Now to Him who is able to do immeasurably more than we ask or imagine, according to his power that is at work within us."

2 Corinthian 4:18 (NIV): "So we fix our eyes not on what is seen, but on what is unseen, since what is seen is temporary, but what is unseen is eternal."

"Lord Jesus, You long for us to hold the things of this world loosely and hang onto You with all our strength and might. We love You, Lord, with our whole heart, and long to do Your will, which at times transcends our reasoning.

Lord, we give You permission to prune us if You find we are not willing to give You control of our lives. Our desire is to be transformed into Your image to reflect Your loving-kindness. We long for Your Kingdom to come and display Your Kingdom's power on earth as it is in heaven.

We choose Your way above our own, examining our motives, making sure they line up with Your will.

We know You have the best for us and will take care of the details of our lives, so we will release ourselves fully into Your care." Amen.

Chapter 7

Resisting Fear-Filled Thoughts!

Throughout the next few months, we continued to have days we would think, "Did we really hear from God, for no person in their right mind would give their home to folks to use and not charge them in this economy?"

Some of our friends thought we were off our rocker; however, we continued to believe God had called us and were steadfast in our position with Christ at the helm.

While the Holy Spirit kept us on course, we were reminded faith takes us in, moves us through, and brings us out to victory. We took notice our emotions were no longer leading, but making it wonderfully clear we had stepped away from the shores of fear and into His waters of rest and peace.

A popular pastor said, "You will know you have a transformed mind when the impossible and illogical seem reasonable and rational."

An epiphany took place during this time. Somehow, it was as if the darkness had rolled away, and the illumination exposed God's truth and light.

I reminded my husband, "If we do not overcome fear, fear will overwhelm us." God has consistently called us to face our fears with courage. We have stood before impossibilities, trembling in our shoes, however, after time, the shaking disappeared, and peace fell on us like leaves falling on an autumn day. We absolutely know God has never been the author of the assaults of intimidation.

We took faith's hand, allowing Him to guide us along the sometimes-bumpy terrain of our new path.

The Lord did provide the finances needed, granting this ministry and missionaries access to our home.

I cannot express the joy we felt in our hearts, knowing we had indeed heard heaven's voice.

We obeyed his instructions and were able to see God's provision time and again.

Mark 10:29-30 (NKJV): "Jesus answered and said, 'Assuredly, I say to you, there is no one who has left house or brothers or sisters or father or mother or wife or children or lands, for My sake and the gospels, who shall not receive a hundredfold now in this time – houses and brothers and sisters and mothers and children and lands, with persecutions – and in the age to come, eternal life.'"

Ephesians 3:16 (NLT): "I pray that from His glorious, unlimited resources He will empower you with inner strength through His Spirit. Then Christ will make His home in your hearts as you trust in Him. Your roots will grow down into God's love and keep you strong."

"Lord Jesus, we thank You for giving us a place to hide when fearful thoughts bombard our minds. You call us away from the safety of the water's edge, where we can feel the sand beneath our feet. The water on which You long for us to step looks terrifying. At times we don't believe we are to walk on top of it, and yet you petition us to come.

May we be a people who dare to face fear's ferocious roar, attempting to intimidate us, holding us back from our destiny. I pray courage rises from within, and our spirit meets face to face with the enemy of our souls, and we crush him with the weight of Your Glory.

When I KNOW who I am and whose I am, nothing will be impossible!" Amen.

Chapter 8

Blessing in Grandpa Bob's Passing

A couple of months after we moved, our very close friend Bob unexpectedly passed away.

We had met Bob at our church a few years earlier, during the Christmas holiday. His wife had died a couple of months earlier, and he was alone.

Bob came for lunch on many days and stayed for dinner as well. We quickly became close, and our kids called him Grandpa Bob. Bob had no grandkids; therefore, it was terrific to have our kids around him. He loved being their grandpa, and it quickly became obvious our friendship was a divine set-up by the Lord.

Bob would come to every soccer practice and game for our son and was well known for bringing his antique cowbell to the games. He also attended every one of our daughter's gymnastics practices.

We loved being around Bob, for his laugh was heartwarming, and his love for our family was priceless.

It was only two months after we moved out of state that Bob came, by train, for a visit and stayed a couple of weeks.

When he arrived, he was not fully healed from foot surgery. We encouraged him to lay low and stay off his foot as much as possible, but he was feisty and there were times we had to insist.

We took him to the train station a couple of weeks later. While traveling home, the train made a stop in a major city, and it was then the employees noticed Bob was not well and moved him safely to a hotel room.

That night, he went to heaven in his sleep. It was not until a few days later we learned that grandpa Bob was gone, because his friend had to track us down.

Then one day, we heard from Bob's brother Jim, letting us know Bob shared the love he had for our family him. Bob had mentioned to his brother Jim, "If anything happens to me, I want my new family to have all of my belongings."

I flew back to our home state with our daughter and cleaned out Bob's tiny, 600-square-foot apartment.

One of the sweetest and most precious things about this story is that 80 percent of Grandpa Bob's belongings, many of which were antique – fit wonderfully into the home we left behind for missionaries. The once-empty home was about to fill up our house with 99 percent of his belongings. It was a 100-year-old Craftsman home – truly a perfect place for Bob's lovely antiques to call home.

Our once empty home left for God's beloved children was now filled with furniture. The living and dining room, along with the bedroom, was filled to the brim.

The kitchen now had kitchenware with a loving history and gorgeous table settings from a heart filled with love. Bob lived on a minimal amount of Social Security but would frequently declare, "I'm the richest man in the world!"

He was an incredibly generous and grateful man, displaying for all to see what being thankful can do to one's countenance.

We knew Bob would be overwhelmed with joy, knowing his belongings blessed these missionary families.

We miss Bob, for he imparted all his love and life to the Lord and us without measure.

John 12:3 (NKJV): "Then Mary took a pound of very costly oil of spikenard, anointed the feet of Jesus, and wiped his feet with her hair. And the house was filled with the fragrance of the oil."

Luke 6:38 (NIV): "Give and it will be given to you. A good measure, pressed down, shaken together and running over, will be poured into your lap. For with the measure you use, it will be measured to you."

As I shared, Bob was one of the most generous people we had ever met. God amazes us still; as we continue to see Bob's generosity touch lives, even though he is gone.

"Lord Jesus, we look to You and recognize what we have here on earth is temporary; therefore, we continually release our lives into Your hands. You are not looking for a laundry list of what we have or have not done, but, instead, lives given to You, relinquished and yielded.

May we recognize that You long for us to be generous with what You have bestowed on us. Freely we have received, and freely we will give.

Lord, we long to please You and spread Your great love and faithfulness to the world around us." Amen.

Chapter 9

Slow Paced-Hair on Fire!

I would like to say we quickly adjusted to our new life in an unfamiliar area, but that would be far from the truth. Our surroundings were, in fact, the extreme opposite of where we had previously lived.

Having no friends or family in our new environment, along with strenuous and sometimes agonizing freeway driving, caused my nerves to become beyond frazzled. There were times I felt exceedingly strained in my emotions along with being stretched in my faith. It got so bad, I was losing hair because my body was feeling the stress.

We needed new drivers' licenses, and the lines were about three to four hour wait time. Signing the kids up for school was also time-consuming, as they need transcripts and information I did not readily have. Our boxes were filled with relevant documents, and it took time to find them.

The officials wanted everything yesterday, and the pressure from it all took my breath away at times.

It was not uncommon to see folks speeding up to 85-plus miles per hour, in 60 miles per hour zones, darting in and out of heavy traffic. They would do the same while navigating the back streets, crossroads, and highways where speeds were posted well below 60 MPH.

There is an old saying: "When in Rome, do as the Romans do." This means it is advisable to follow the conventions of the area you are residing in or visiting.

Well, I knew THAT would not pertain to me, as I could not see myself driving like Parnelli Jones, the famous race-car driver.

We had moved from grass, acre lots, loads of trees, and copious lakes and saltwater. Our state was filled with mountains and rolling hills surrounding us, with only two major freeways.

Now we were living in a state with few trees, little grass, no mountains, and hundreds of interstates, along with extreme pollution and millions of cars. With every driver appearing to be in a hurry, it took its toll and wore down my nerves.

I've lived my entire life with continual optimism, no matter how bleak and difficult the circumstances were. Clearly I was undergoing a trial; one I was determined to pass through gleefully.

Thankfully, God was faithful and continued showing me ways to overcome; and overcome, I did.

I would regularly joke with folks declaring, "On the eighth day, God must have created GPS navigators." I could not get my bearings when finding my way around our new surroundings and was easily lost in the vastness of this County.

Over the years, when I've found myself uncomfortable and anxious, when in a new environment, God's tender hand brought me to His side, where I found peace.

I want to be willing to step away from the anxious feelings and step into a place of quiet trust where the Holy Spirit is waiting to bring His comfort. It is there I continually find the rest I am seeking.

When I allow my mind, will, and emotions to lead me, I will feel overwhelmed. There have been areas in my life needing a touch from heaven, and thankfully Jesus has not let me remain in those unhealthy patterns of living.

Our move to a new state clearly made me feel uncomfortable, but I found myself being grateful. Those unhealed places within came bubbling to the surface, and God brought much-needed healing to my soul.

I now know it is crucial I examine my unhealthy reactions. Each of those times, when displaying my agitation and discomfort, the Holy Spirit is inviting me to receive healing in areas of brokenness.

My heart cries out to Jesus, allowing His touch to restore my soul. God earnestly waits, longing to replace the cyclical progression of poor behavioral traits with healthy ones.

Malachi 4:2 (NKJV): "But to you who fear my name the sun of righteousness shall arise with healing in his wings; and you shall go out and grow fat like stall-fed calves."

2 Corinthians 5:17 (NKJV): "Therefore, if anyone is in Christ, he is a new creation; old things have passed away; behold, all things have become new."

Psalms 51:6 (NKJV): "Behold, You desire truth in the inward parts, and in the hidden part, thou shall make me know wisdom."

Proverbs 8:11 (NKJV): "For wisdom is better than rubies, and all the things one may desire are not to be compared."

"Lord, we recognize, when following You, nothing is repeated. You make all things new and remind us being transformed into Your image is a process.

As your word says, Matthew 5:8 (NIV), 'Blessed are the pure in heart, for they will see God.'

We acknowledge, Lord, we do not have pure hearts, for our hearts can be deceitful, and not easily trusted.

You summon us to wait patiently, while we will submit to the preparations and development. Knowing You move us from glory to glory, causes our road to be filled with joy and a future bright." Amen.

Chapter 10

Jesus and Our Boats

We found a place to fellowship with believers near our home and immediately became involved.

My husband and I believe it is vital to serve wherever we worship within the four walls of the body of Christ Jesus.

We rolled up our sleeves, making ourselves available to the church leadership. They, in turn, gave us the position of Greeter Leaders. A pastor handed us a list of approximately 50 volunteers for our team. We attended church on Wednesdays and Sundays, arriving early and staying late.

On a Wednesday evening, after leaving the service, Steve said, "I wonder why our boat has not sold?"

It had been several months, with not one inquiry, and my sweet hubby was growing anxious. I responded to his seeming inquiry: "It's God's boat and God's money. I am confident He has a buyer, one who will come forward in due time."

When moving away, we not only left behind our home but also a beautiful boat named Ephraim. Putting her up for sale before heading out was a difficult decision. Still, we had high hopes someone would purchase her and be willing to continue the restoration process.

Our Ephraim was a 46-foot Chris Craft classic wooden vessel, which we had already poured hundreds of hours into. She required tender, loving care because the previous owner had neglected her. To bring her closer to her original condition, would require hundreds more hours, inside and out. Before moving, we had only begun the process of restoration.

After I let him know God was on His throne and all would be well, he quickly responded, "God just told me, if we buy a boat here, the other one will sell."

I immediately gasped and replied, "Write that down because that was not you; it has to be God." Being married to a logical and analytical engineer has been fun. I have watched him release more and more of his logic and reason, to the Lord. It has been a joy to watch God show my hubby a different Kingdom, demonstrating His power. I knew my husband would not have come up with a solution for selling our boat, which sounded utterly irrational in the natural realm. It was evident to us both, God had imparted His idea, and we were on board.

Steve and I were absolutely confident God revealed the answer to our ongoing petition for our boat to sell. The funny thing is, we had absolutely NO desire for another boat!

Romans 12:2 (NLT): "Don't copy the behavior and customs of this world but let God transform you into a new person by changing the way you think. Then you will know the will of God for you, which is good and pleasing and perfect."

After reading this scripture for years, we have concluded that Jesus sometimes takes a long time to act suddenly, and this appeared to be the case when selling our vessel.

Since my husband and I were certain, God spoke, even though we did not want another boat, we moved ahead eager to respond to the Lord and begin our search.

Seeing many boats and spending days on end searching for the perfect vessel, we got frustrated and discouraged. Each boat we thought we might be able to afford was falling apart or filled with mildew and mold. We could not see ourselves owning another project boat.

Now, remember, we were paying a mortgage on our home, allowing a ministry to use it at no cost, paying for the rental we lived in, and paying a boat payment and moorage where we moved from.

Our rental home was located in one of the most expensive places in the nation.

Looking at our finances, buying another boat did not make sense, and glancing at our bank account, it made less sense; as it appeared, we had no funds to purchase another boat.

Because we knew God sent us, we were confident and held great peace, believing God would make it happen. It was evident the only possible way to own another boat was a supernatural move of God.

Since God said to buy another vessel, we said, YES, but honestly, from time to time, we would share our thoughts with one another, and we both would say to the Lord, "Are You SURE you know what You are doing?"

I remember laughing at myself for asking the Creator of the Universe if He knew what He was doing!

We reminded one another our thoughts were bringing confusion, and the Lord was not the author of the chaotic dialog we were wrestling with.

We continued our search but, ultimately, found nothing. One evening, we prayed, asking, "God, have we seen the boat you want us to purchase?"

He said, "YES!"

We scratched our heads, thinking, WHAT? We had not seen a boat we even liked, so this added to our dilemma and feeling bewildered..

We decided to call our pastor, who was also our mentor, letting him know about our situation and asked for prayer and wisdom. He responded immediately: "Why are you looking for a boat you can afford, why not look for a boat which requires you to be dependent on God?"

To this day, he said he had never mentioned anything like that before and to this day he has not made a comment similar. He knew it was God, and we agreed.

We began looking for boats which were way beyond our pay grade and unattainable without

God's intervention. Our explorations continued for a couple of weeks, driving to distant marinas, checking out boats with Tim, our salesmen. We shared while on our drives to check out vessels, all the miracles our Savior was doing.

After we had exhausted all avenues, our salesman, Tim, called and said, "I have one more boat to show you." He had us follow him in our car to the final boat. When we saw it, we began laughing uncontrollably.

We had admired this exact boat while driving through the neighborhood waterway a month earlier.

My hubby and I had commented on the beauty of the boat when driving by weeks previous and did not know it was for sale. Before exiting our car, my husband and I shared, "Only God could cause this to happen, surely this was God alone!"

The vessel's name was "Love U 2." Unlike the boat back home, it needed no immediate work, as the owners had just spent $40,000 on improvements.

We felt wondrous peace, and with a name like Love U 2, we could not help but feel God's approval. It was clear to us God was giving His nod over the purchase of her, and therefore, we moved forward.

1 Corinthians 1:27 (KJV): "But God has chosen the foolish things of the world to confound the wise; and God chose the weak things of the world to confound the things which are mighty."

Isaiah 55:8 (NIV): "For My thoughts are not your thoughts, neither are your ways My ways, declares the Lord."

"Lord Jesus, thank You for knowing who we are, falling short of the faith You have called us to, and most likely chuckling when we fail to see You working in our lives. We desire to walk by faith and not by sight, and yet at times, we do.

Lord, You are so gracious to forgive us time and again. It is Your love which never gives up, never stops pursuing us, relentlessly chases after us.

May we stop in our stride to outrun the enemy, recognizing YOU and not him. We long to walk in Your Spirit realm, that no voice of the enemy can convince us we've lost when You have let us know we have won." Amen.

Chapter 11

God's Order, Not Ours!

You'll remember, the Lord told us to buy a boat before the other one sold, and if we did the one we own previously would sell.

Here is our story of how God turned the impossible to possible.

Less than a week after we had purchased our new boat, someone answered the ad we'd placed on Craigslist in the city and state from which we had moved. A couple who responded to our ad told us they were moving to the very same region we had moved from and wanted to purchase the boat to live on. Again we found ourselves pondering how this could not be a coincidence. Every fiber of our being was feeling great excitement and anticipation because we knew God was once again up to something amazing.

They shared where they currently lived, and it was extremely close to where we were living.

The Lord continued to surprise us with the way He answered our prayers. We kept reminding ourselves God merely wanted us to trust Him. What were the chances we would find a buyer for our boat in the town near the one we had just moved to? Honestly, it seemed unreal!

We both knew God's handwriting was all over the upcoming meeting. We love the scripture, which says, "With God, ALL things are possible!"

We set up a time to meet our potential buyers in a restaurant 30 minutes from our home.

At our initial meeting, I remember thinking, "This couple surely can't be serious about living on a boat." The lower portion of the gentleman's leg was missing and had a prosthetic. Navigating the steep stairs and the fly-bridge ladder on our vessel would be super tricky.

Before we began our discussion, we shared about Jesus and our story of God moving us away from our home state. They eagerly wanted to hear more.

As we shared, they leaned in, as if they were hanging on our words, welcoming our prayers about their upcoming move.

After our prayer and listening to their reasoning as to why they wanted to live on a boat, we found ourselves discouraging them from purchasing it.

"You DO know how chilly it is up north, and it will be colder living on a boat in the winter!" I declared.

They would not back away from their desire to purchase the boat, even though we shared our concerns; therefore, we moved forward, requiring a contract and 20 percent down.

"Buy a boat here, and the one you left behind will sell," the Lord had said. There we were, living in God's prophetic word for us.

Within the first year, the buyers had to give back our vessel, as she had encountered circumstances at her place of employment, which compelled her to step away.

We listed our boat again and began moving forward with finding another buyer. Within a couple of weeks, we had another offer, though this time, the prospective buyers lived in the state from which we had moved. Eventually, we agreed on terms, and once again, we required 20 percent down. They happily accepted.

The new buyers were woodworkers and had restored a mansion in a city in our home state. We were confident our boat would be safe in their hands. By the end of our contract, the work they had accomplished was breathtaking.

More money was made than initially planned, and this meant more to give back to God.

When we live each day operating out of His Kingdom realm, miraculous and supernatural doors have opened. We have seen Jesus create dreams out of the dust, displaying to my family, each time we are obedient, favor is uncovered in the natural realm.

Our boat sold twice because we submitted to His plans, and we love to point to Him as the Author, not ourselves. When we had initially purchased our boat back home, her name was "Blue Moon."

The Lord told us to rename her and call her "Ephraim." In Hebrew, Ephraim means, a double portion, double blessing, and fruitfulness! We serve an awesome God, don't we!

We believe we must take great care of what God has given, and when we are faithful, He will increase in every way in and through us. Whether the increase comes in the form of God's presence, financially, or otherwise, it matters not to us but only that he is smiling over our lives.

Luke 6:38 (NIV): "Give and it will be given to you; a good measure, pressed down, shaken together and running over, will be poured into your lap. For with the measure you use, it will be measured to you."

Matthew 21:22 (NIV): "If you believe, you will receive whatever you ask for in prayer."

Isaiah 30:18-20 (AMPC): "And therefore the Lord (earnestly) waits (expecting, looking, and longing) to be gracious to you; and therefore He lifts Himself up, that He may have mercy on you and show loving-kindness to you. For the Lord is a God of justice. Blessed (happy, fortunate, to be envied) are all those who (earnestly) wait for Him, who expect and look and long for Him (for His victory, His favor, His love, His peace, His joy, and His matchless, unbroken companionship)."

"Lord, we thank You for Your flawless word, full of integrity, backed by Your unfailing love.

May we be a people who respond to Your call, when the way appears risky and the path on which You have us doesn't seem secure.

Let us remember, we did hear Your voice, and the confusion we may feel is not of You. At times, when we question ourselves and even You, we will stay the course, and watch You bring about what You have promised. Success is guaranteed when we place our trust in You." Amen.

Chapter 12

Lord of the Harvest and Healing

One of my favorite things is to share my love for Jesus and all He has done.

The neighborhood in which we had rented our home was filled with folks from all around the world. Within the community we lived in, we met people from Asia, Iran, India, Africa, Mexico, Spain, and more.

I LOVED being among such amazing folks, learning about their culture, and admiring their commitment to family.

I became acquainted with a couple of women whose kids attended our daughter's elementary school.

In particular, one woman loved hanging out with me, and I enjoyed our time together as well. She was Muslim and shared what she believed. I, being a Christian, shared my beliefs with her.

She would invariably say, "You are an angel. I just love being in your presence." I knew it was Jesus and was hoping she did as well.

One day, a mother from our daughter's school remarked on a long black suede blazer I was wearing. She went on and on about it, asking me where I had purchased it and let me know she wanted to buy one.

We were attending a school in a high-end neighborhood; therefore, I decided not to tell her I had purchased it at a thrift store, thinking she might find me a bit odd.

I did chuckle inside, as I loved being frugal, shopping at stores, where I could find treasures someone had deemed useless. Purchasing clothes at bargain prices, knowing someone else had paid a fortune for them, made me smile.

The Lord reminded me of what He did when I prayed over a pillowcase while visiting my client in Hospice when I had my hair salon. Her daughter called and asked if I would go to the hospital and pray with her, letting me know she loved to hear my stories of faith.

While I was on my way to see her, the Lord had me stop and purchase a satin pillowcase and pray over it, reminding me of the book of Acts chapter 19:12 NIV "So that even the handkerchiefs and aprons that had touched him were taken to the sick, and their illnesses were cured and the evil spirits left them."

When I walked into her room, I could see a drastic change from the last time I had seen her, for she now was thin, gaunt, and without color.

I placed the pillowcase on her pillow and prayed for her. My visit was not long, but I knew God had done something supernaturally special in her heart.

Two days later, I received a call from her daughter, letting me know her mom was home and healed! I was jumping up and down, inside and out, saying, "Praise Jesus!"

Recalling that event, I became excited at the thought of anointing and praying over my black jacket the sweet parent had loved; and gifting it to her.

I love to watch the pages of each day unfold before me, revealing God's plan to bring about His will. I will forever remember the smile on the woman's face when I handed her my beautiful jacket and the warmth in my heart for having obeyed God.

She was thrilled to receive my gift, and I was excited she would wear the anointed jacket, knowing God would do what He had promised.

When the "bird flu" was making its rounds, the following year, I did what I love to do: I purchased cleaning products and cleaned the classroom, praying over each child's desk. I placed anointing oil in the products and cleaned each desk and table at the end of every day. I was told my daughter's classroom was the healthiest one that year.

The Lord had me purchase gift cards, flowers, and thank you cards to share with folks who worked at the school's front office, along with teachers, janitors, librarians, and P.T.A. members. We were excited to display God's love, with acts of kindness and words of encouragement.

I would fill bags with bath salts, body lotion, and winter neck wraps to bring warmth. I prayed over each item, believing God would supernaturally touch them and change their lives.

Flowers and gift cards were given to bank tellers, cashiers in the stores I frequented, or even occasionally a homeless person.

I would write scriptures inside cards, with words of appreciation, and often included a gift card. When I arrived with my gift, they were shocked and pleased.

I long to impart a lasting impression, one which leaves the recipient wondering who they were in the presence of, hoping they saw Jesus in me.

What I found interesting was most of those who received were more interested in reading the card. The gift I gave them seemed to almost go unnoticed. The Lord showed me that His children are starved for words of affirmation, recognition, and love.

If I accidentally missed an appointment, I would go back later with an apology, along with a card in hand, flowers, or a gift card.

Many folks were caught off-guard by the fact someone had taken the time to complete an act of kindness.

The Lord placed on my heart the desire to demonstrate His loving-kindness toward others.

I believe we are to be Jesus to those around us. Jesus left behind signs, wonders, and miracles, and He instructed us to do the same.

Acts 19:12 (NLT): "When handkerchiefs or aprons that had merely touched his skin were placed on sick people, they were healed of their diseases, and evil spirits were expelled."

Acts 20:35 (NIV): "In everything I did; I showed you that by this kind of hard work we must help the weak, remembering the world, for the Lord Jesus said, 'It is more blessed to give than to receive.'"

Hebrews 13:16 (NIV): "And do not forget to do good and to share with others, for with such sacrifices, God is pleased."

Luke 6:38 (NIV): "Give, and it will be given to you. A good measure, pressed down, shaken together and running over, will be poured into your lap. For with the measure you use, it will be measured to you."

"Lord Jesus, we look to You, and learn of You, for You are meek, lowly, and humble of heart. Let us serve You always with integrity and humility, acknowledging our need for our Savior.

When we are out in the workplace and our communities, I pray we leave behind a mark of heaven on earth. May Your Kingdom come and, Your will be done on earth as it is in heaven.

Lord, we love bringing to earth what is held in heaven, allowing praise to continually flow out of us, with lives worshipping you and hearts full of thanksgiving lifted to Your Throne." Amen.

Chapter 13

Going After the One

Since Jesus brought me into His grace and mercy, years ago, I find myself living in perpetual gratitude. I knew the life I was living before Christ wasn't "life" at all.

Had I kept going in the direction I was heading, I would not have been alive much longer. Each day I awake, I am beyond grateful to my Savior. I love to reach out and share God's love with others.

This love I have cannot stay silent; I am compelled to share my faith in Jesus, and I do.

This next story is of a young lady whom I will call Sheila. I met her while I waited for my daughter outside her kindergarten classroom.

Sheila was stunningly gorgeous, with a curvy, statuesque body covered in tattoos. All the women stayed clear of her, most likely because her beauty intimidated them. I knew in my spirit, I was to do the opposite and move toward her with God's love.

I began chatting with Sheila each day while waiting for my daughter to be released from school. Our daughters were in the same class, and I saw that as an opening into her life to bring God's love. Each day I approached her and began our conversations by asking questions and finding what we had in common.

There was an age difference, as Sheila was young enough to be my daughter, but God has been good to me throughout my life, giving me ease when speaking with strangers. She shared with me openly, letting me know she was living with her boyfriend and was pregnant.

The way she carried herself, I sensed she knew her appearance made others uncomfortable. Even so, she was warm and friendly when I approached.

Over time, I felt the Lord nudge my heart to host a baby shower for Sheila. I invited women from our church and some of the moms from our daughter's class.

Sheila came with her boyfriend and daughter. Our home was filled with loving women who literally showered her with God's love and lots of baby gifts.

I know Jesus touched Sheila's heart that day, along with her boyfriend and daughter. We met up many times in the year I spent with her. She shared stories of her broken, dysfunctional childhood, and I shared how God had healed me from my own.

Sheila knew I was a believer, as I shared my stories of God's love and faithfulness toward me over the years, and she always seemed eager to hear.

We invited her and her family to church and continued our friendship for a while. I believe we made an impact on their lives, and hope to this day that they are kept by God's grace.

Colossians 3:12 (NIV): "Therefore, as God's chosen people, holy and dearly loved, clothe yourselves with compassion, kindness, humility, gentleness, and patience."

John 15:12 (NIV): "My command is this: Love each other as I have loved you.

As we open the page of today, we begin acknowledging You Lord. We see open signs and closed signs, in the Spirit realm, as we navigate through. Some read, 'Enter in, and some say, Exit.'"

Which one do we choose to access, and which one do we leave through? You Lord light up our path if confusion tries to cloud it and bring clarity to questions when our minds seem cluttered.

You are the Keeper of our way, the Lifter of our heads, the Voice calling us out, and the Hand leading us in.

You're the Preparer of our day, the Announcer of Good News, the Shoulder on which we lean, and our Strength to make us new. May we experience a continual outpouring of Your joy, and Your matchless power, to keep us in perfect peace. If our enemies appear to be closing in, surrounding us with their weapons, You dispatch Heavenly Hosts and remind us that we're hidden within Your Shadow, and tucked beneath Your Wings. May our lives be filled with monuments, telling stories, like the one I just shared, of our days containing Your grace and favor!" Amen.

Chapter 14

Friendships and HIV Healed

As I shared earlier, one of our pastors asked us to lead the greeter's team at our large church.

There were two-morning services and one evening service. Because my husband was at work all day, and the kids were in school, I decided to take on the leadership role, overseeing approximately 50-plus greeters.

We began meeting many folks from the team, and I formed a few relationships with some of the women. I'd like to share a testimony of a specific woman I will call Rita, who was a greeter. I will be sharing about one specific evening, while cutting her and her daughter's hair, that changed my life and theirs.

After Rita learned I was a hairstylist, she asked if she could be my client. Rita let me know she needed a new stylist, and I told her I would be happy to be hers. After selling my salon, I kept my license current and was able to continue cutting hair now and then.

Over time, we developed a friendship. We shared stories about our love for Jesus and the many miracles He had done. She called me two days before Christmas and let me know she and her daughter needed haircuts.

At the time, her daughter, who I will call Sam, was homeless and living on the streets. She was also HIV-positive. "If you don't want to cut her hair, I understand," my friend said. I knew immediately was she was referring to.

Throughout my career, I had worked with men and women who had lost their lives to AIDS; therefore, I understood what she was saying. She and I knew it could be dangerous if I cut her daughter's hair and had a cut on my finger. The virus could be transmitted to me, infecting me for a lifetime.

When she asked though, I boldly declared, "Of course, I would love to cut her hair; bring her along, and God will heal her!" Throughout my life, I had seen an abundance of miracles and knew nothing was impossible for God – not even AIDS!

She asked that I not mention she had spoken to me about her daughter's illness, and I agreed. I had a hair salon chair and a large mirror placed in our tiny garage. When they came that evening, I ushered them into my makeshift space, equipped for a night of sharing Jesus and cutting hair.

The Lord had me begin trimming my friend's hair first, while her daughter sat and waited.

God had a strategy, and I was all in. I knew what He had in mind, which was genius, of course. I know there is wonder-working power in our testimonies, to overcome the enemy, and God wanted her to listen to me recounting my past victories.

I believe when we share our stories of Jesus, He miraculously shows up, and faith is released. When faith is released, it changes the atmosphere and allows the hearer to accept a miracle.

When I was a young woman, I was involved in drugs and alcohol. It was my meager attempt to dull the pain of my past, allowing me momentary slices of times to not feel the sting of the pain I was in.

As I shared, Sam was all ears, and eager to hear what God had done in my life. It was an extraordinarily powerful time!

I was transparent while sharing some of my own life struggles before knowing Jesus, letting her know she wasn't alone.

I had been snipping away at her mom's hair for about 10 minutes. Suddenly, the daughter stood up and declared, "I am going to have a cigarette, Mom. You can tell her!"

She walked out the door, and I said, "PRAISE GOD!"

The POWER of God descended, enveloping our little garage, and I immediately dropped to the ground, unable to stand.

The overwhelming presence of the Holy Spirit lifted my heart and spirit, taking me into God's chambers of compassion and love.

We both sat, tears streaming down our faces, our bodies limp under the weight of God's Glory.

As we sat weeping, me on the cement floor, and she in the salon chair, we recognized Jesus was present, wanting to do the miraculous.

His presence engulfed the small area, turning it into what I imagined the Holy of Holies might be like.

While we were concealed in God's Spirit, Sam came back into the garage and asked, "Why are you both sobbing?"

I collected myself, standing to my feet, and held her in my arms, declaring, "You are healed!"

She surprised me by joyfully proclaimed, "I KNOW I am healed!" That was 10 years ago, and Sam is alive and completely healed to this day – whole, healed, and serving Jesus! She has a beautiful young daughter as well.

Psalm 107:20 (NIV): "He sent out his word and healed them; he rescued them from the grave."

Isaiah 41:10 (NIV): "So do not fear, for I am with you; do not be dismayed, for I am your God. I will strengthen you and help; I will uphold you with my righteous right hand."

Had I been frightened about contracting HIV, I would have declined when asked to cut her hair.

"Lord Jesus, we want to consistently respond to Your request, and step out in faith each time You ask, and when we do, our lives are changed. Faith is trusting in

the integrity of who You are, Lord. You are good, and our enemy is NOT.

Satan comes to kill, steal, and destroy; it's not the job description of You, our Messiah.

You gave us power and authority over the evil one, which means the devil has no authority, and we have it all; unless we give him our authority.

We remember Your word, which says the weapons of our warfare are not carnal. Therefore, we have supernatural weapons, given by You, to destroy the works of the devil.

Let us use them, and not let them sit in our closet, untouched. We must put on our armor and take up our Swords and Shields, go forth in faith to destroy the works of our enemy!" Amen.

Chapter 15

Boat and Baby Time

God reminded us the boats we'd purchased over the years are tools for sharing his love with others. I reminded my husband, "We are not here for us, we are here for HIM!"

With our previous boat, and now with this one, we allowed the Lord to direct us toward those he wanted to encourage. We are acutely aware of the Lord's desire for us to be His mouthpiece and hands.

We make it a habit to remind ourselves we are not here on earth for us; we are here for HIM!

We made preparations for an outing on our boat, with about 20 greeters. What was delightful about living in a sunny state is that we did not have to pray for sunshine, it was sunny most the time, unlike where we previously lived.

We made sure those invited on our outing were comfortable on the water, with no susceptibility to seasickness. Where we had lived previously, the saltwater was pretty calm most days; it wasn't the coastal waters. The ocean where our new boat was, however, was another story. The ocean was unpredictable, and winds could rise up quickly, so being prepared was a must.

Throughout the day, I was able to share many of our testimonies. One story in particular, which I share to this day, is God enabling me to give birth to my two children, even though doctors said it was not possible.

At 20 years old, I'd had my left ovary and tube removed because of endometriosis. Endometriosis causes sterility and can be deadly.

I have an arsenal of stories about the women I've met and shared my testimony with. Over the past 17 years, I have shared my testimony with women who were told by physicians they were infertile … Then, suddenly, by the grace of God, they conceived. I've shared with nurses in the hospital when they saw I was pregnant and knew my age.

"You're in your forties and have a young child," they would proclaim. Two of the women nurses asked me to pray, and I did. Later, I found out they had conceived!

Our neighbor let me know she had tried for years to conceive. We had her and her husband for dinner, and I shared my story, and we prayed. She became pregnant the next month. I could go on and on about my baby testimony releasing faith toward others.

During the day on our boat, one woman, whom I will call Cindy, piped up and declared, "Will you and your husband pray for us when we get back to the dock?"

She went on: "We have tried for seven years to conceive and have not been able." After we arrived at the dock, and almost everyone had left, we prayed for Cindy and her husband.

The following month, she was pregnant. Today, they have three kids. It's beautiful watching women, who long to have a baby, grow in expectancy and excitement while sharing my testimonies.

Friends, when we share testimonies they release faith, changing the atmosphere. Expectancy replaces doubt and hopelessness, and our faith has room to grow.

Hope attracts what it anticipates! When one hears the testimonies of others receiving what was impossible, faith is supernaturally released and charges the atmosphere.

When hope and faith rise to the Lord's throne room, saints of God receive what they believed and stood for.

A couple of months later, Cindy brought a friend and her husband to my home. They, too, were unable to conceive. I shared some of our powerful testimonies and prayed for them, and of course, a few months later, we received word she, too, was pregnant.

To this day, I have shared my testimony with well over 20 women. They have received, by faith, what they believed for.

We love to share and watch God do his thing. Not me, NEVER me, only Jesus!

Hebrews 11:1 (NIV): "Now faith is the confidence in what we hope for, and assurance of about what we do not see."

Romans 4:20 (NLT): "Abraham never wavered in believing God's promise. In fact, his faith grew stronger and in this he brought glory to God."

Hebrews 11:11 (NLT): "It was by faith that even Sarah was able to have a child, though she was barren and was too old. She believed that God would keep His promise."

"Lord, we know faith can rise while we wait on You. We also know we can lose hope in the waiting.

Forgive us, Lord, for the times when we've thrown in the towel on our dreams, if you will, and given up believing our prayer will be answered.

Thank You, Lord, for continuing to remind us that You birthed our desires and placed them within our hearts, and that You have every intention of fulfilling them.

May we rise up and take a stand, where faith can grow wings and we can watch You perform what You have promised." Amen.

Chapter 16

Stop Signs – Red Curbs – Courage

One morning, while dropping off our daughter at her elementary school, I cautioned her about an area that needed crossing before entering the school grounds.

It was a dangerous portion of the sidewalk. With sandwich board signs blocking the entrance, these signs let parents know the parking lot was not to be accessed during school hours.

We soon found out these signs held no significance, as each morning and afternoon, parents would move the signs and drive right in. One parent would park their car in front of the standing billboards, remove them and head on through. A parade of other parents quickly followed suit.

One morning, as it was drizzling, I sat in my car, waiting for our daughter to safely cross. Then, out of the corner of my eye, I saw a vehicle quickly accelerate, entering the area where my daughter was about to cross.

As fast as I could, I hopped out of my car and screamed at my daughter, "STOP, don't go!" She stopped short of being run over. I ran to her and held her, shaking like a rattlesnake tail. She did not know what was about to happen, which was just as well.

Later that night, I shared with my husband all that had taken place. We had a conversation about how God might want to use me to remedy the hazardous situation.

I scheduled an appointment with the principal later that week. After introducing myself, I let her know what had happened with our daughter, sharing the treacherous ongoing situation at the parking lot entrance.

Ours was not the only horror story she had heard. She said, "This area has been a problem for many years!"

"I'd like to be a part of the solution and not just someone who complains," I declared!

The principal was shocked at first because most people apparently had complained without a solution.

The principal handed me a lime green vest and stop paddle, asking if I would volunteer as their official safety officer.

I knew this was an opening from the Lord, so I happily grabbed my new attire.

I let her know I would be there each morning and afternoon, ensuring the kids' safety.

I remember thinking, 'Why would parents of elementary school children not drive cautiously, preventing any accidents or deaths?"

After a few days in my newfound career, I had the opportunity to meet and speak with many parents who thanked me for being there. I had several conversations with dads and moms who let me know they had experienced near-tragedies at the same location.

Now I had first-hand experience with parents whose behavior was off the charts, and jaw dropping. Alas, now I knew how to pray. Their maniacal behavior was outrageous at best – attempting to run me over while calling me names.

Thankfully the Lord reminded me I was not wrestling with flesh and blood, and what I was going through was a spiritual battle. (Ephesians 6:12)

I want to share a story about one person in particular whom God got a hold of. I'll refer to him as Bill.

One sunny afternoon, working in my new position as a safety officer, Bill displayed his frustration.

Bill decided to park his van in front of the sandwich boards, refusing to leave.

He literally turned off the ignition while sitting in his vehicle, thereby blocking the area that kids needed to cross. After school was out, I made my way to the principal's office, letting her know about this man's disturbing behavior and seeking advice on how to deal with him.

She let me know Bill and his family were having a rough go of it. He had no job, and his wife had severe health issues.

This information helped me have compassion. The next day, when I saw him, I spoke about why I was there. "Hey Bill, my name is Sherrie, my daughter was almost run over Monday. I am from a state where kids are picked up and brought to school on buses."

I went on, "I spoke to the principal, and she asked me to be here because this is a dangerous area. My only motivation is to make sure kids can cross safely."

Bill's intense behavior lightened up after I shared. Much to my surprise, the following morning, Bill was wearing a lime green vest, ready to jump in and help me!

I loved seeing his willingness to participate, being a part of a solution, and not a danger to others. Other parents offered to help as well; however, I knew more was required to bring about a lasting solution.

I prayed with my husband, asking the Lord for solutions. God placed on my heart the need for me to visit the city engineers and the local police.

I have never been comfortable speaking to professionals who are experts in their particular field, so this was a stretch for me.

Typically, I am somewhat timid when I am with folks when not knowing about their area of expertise.

I was trembling, quite a bit, at just the thought of speaking to a sergeant at the police station.

Then I began shaking, thinking of speaking to an engineer for the city.

I remembered reading a particular question one month before, which caused a paradigm shift in my approach to intimidating situations.

"If there is one thing I would be doing, if I were not afraid, fear has influenced my destiny," the author wrote.

THAT was a compelling statement – one that caused me to pause and examine my life.

Friends, I know God is the author of faith and not fear.

I knew I had to overcome the obstacle of anxiety and visit these folks, as they held keys to bring about change.

I wanted to watch God create a positive outcome for this school and its young students.

Over the next couple of months, I visited both places, speaking to a police sergeant and an engineer who oversaw the schools in their city.

They were aware of the existing issues and kept letting me know there was not much they would be able to do. I walked away discouraged on a few occasions, but not defeated.

I believed with my entire heart, God would move this seemingly immovable mountain with persistence and prayer.

Daily, I embraced, with passion, my appointed job as a crossing guard. Nearly every day, I would hear from folks about their near-death experiences.

After many prayers and visits to the local authorities, God opened the doors, creating a way where there appeared to be no possible way.

The principal had said the problem had gone on for over 10 years and she was discouraged, but she knew I was a woman of faith with the backing of heaven.

Stop signs were placed where they had never existed, and curbs were redone where the paint had faded.

I loved that it was now clear to the lawbreakers that they would be ticketed if they chose to disobey.

The elementary school principal and many parents were thrilled to see the change, and we gave God the glory.

Steve and I believe in leaving behind signs, wonders, and miracles, just as God shared in His word. We got to see actual signs this time, as memorials for the Lord and His provision.

Stop signs now stand erect, and curbs once faded were now bright red.

I knew God had a solution to the ongoing danger presenting itself at our daughter's school. We believe in the power of prayer – praying in agreement while waiting on the Lord to bring about a lasting solution.

Mark 11:24 (NIV): "Therefore I tell you, whatever you ask for in prayer, believe that you have received it, and it will be yours."

Isaiah 30:18 (AMP): "And therefore the Lord (earnestly) waits (expecting, looking and longing) to be gracious to you; and therefore He lifts Himself up, that He may have mercy on you and show loving kindness to you. For the Lord is a God of justice. Blessed (happy, fortunate, to be envied) are all those who wait for Him (for His victory, His favor, His love, His peace, His joy, and His matchless, unbroken companionship)!"

"Lord Jesus, we ask for forgiveness for giving away the authority you've given us.

You gave us power and authority over the enemy and yet we often unknowingly give it back to him. You quickened my spirit, calling me to be courageous and to go before the police sergeant and city engineers, reminding me You had it all handled.

We strip the enemy of ANY authority we handed over to him, and we ask you to destroy the demonic activity that took place because of our unbelief. The lawlessness that took place on the school grounds, with nobody speaking up, should not be. We must rise up and face the enemy and allow you to use us.

Lord, thank You for giving us Grace to have another chance to set the record straight, making right the wrongs, and taking back what was stolen!

Let Your Kingdom come and Your will be done on earth as it is in Heaven. You reign, Jesus, and You are the Victor, Lord; Triumphant, and the One Who DOMINATES!" Amen.

Chapter 17

Don't Touch,
Just Call Out Jesus

The Lord took me in and through three incredible experiences, showing His vauable spiritual truths.

He filled me with His wisdom and power to overcome painful struggles where I found myself stuck.

I asked the Lord what He wanted to reveal, causing ease in my journey, with far less pain and more breakthrough.

More specifically, I prayed for detailed strategies and open doors to new paths through some of my repeated mistakes, which caused much frustration.

These lessons were life-changing.

My hope is that they will encourage you and perhaps catapult you out of any cyclical patterns.

Lesson #1

Our son was entering his senior year when we moved out of state.

By the time we made it to our God-given destination, all the seniors at our son's high school had attained their schedules for the year. This meant our son had slim pickings.

Because we had arrived late in the summer, he had little to choose from, and he needed an English credit to graduate.

The only opening was a British Literature class. My first impactful lesson came from this class and its teacher.

Our son was gifted in English and American Lit, leaving our home state with an A+ in both junior semesters.

He wrote his first paper for his British Lit class and shared it with his dad and me one morning.

I remember saying, "You know plagiarism is illegal, correct?"

I was half-joking, as I knew he was gifted, and this paper was written by someone who was.

He replied, "MOM, I wrote that paper myself!" His dad and I were very impressed with the quality of his work.

As he walked through the door after school, I asked him how his teacher liked his finished assignment. He let us know his teacher held up his paper in front of the entire class and declared, "I am using Jordan's work to show you all what not to do. This is horrible work – completely wrong and literally stupid!"

Yes, in front of the entire class, this teacher had thoroughly embarrassed him. I had a friend of his who was in the same classroom attest to her horrific behavior.

His dad and I were speechless. "What kind of high school teacher displays this kind of horrifying behavior?" we asked ourselves.

Another month went by, and another problematic paper was due in my son's British Literature class. I offered my support, helping where I could, as I enjoyed writing and thought I may be able to add some insight. I spent hours assisting my son, being reasonably sure my input would be helpful, as I, too, had done well in English.

We poured ourselves into this assignment and were confident the teacher would be more than pleased.

A few days after he turned in the assignment, I received an e-mail from his teacher, explaining our son was utterly inept and needed tutoring.

Once again, we were shocked – only this time, I was offended because I had helped.

I had truly believed she was going to give the paper a rave review, and I wondered how I could have been so wrong. I wrote back and let her know I wanted to meet with her.

I was hoping to gain insight into her requirements and discover how our son was so far off the mark.

On the day of my scheduled meeting with our son's teacher, I had my six-year-old daughter in tow. We walked toward the school offices. Before we could ascend the stairs, a fight was about to break out between two young students.

A crowd had gathered to watch, and I pondered how to navigate the area with my daughter's hand clutching mine. I walked smack into the middle of them, looking both students in the eye and boldly announced, "You are NOT going to do this right now, are you, not in front of my daughter?"

They stopped and walked away. We moved past the crowd and headed up another flight of stairs to the main office.

In front of us, scaling the stairs was the first adult I had seen since arriving on the school campus.

"Are you a teacher?" I asked while climbing the steps, still shaking from my unexpected conflict.

He answered, "Why, yes, I am. Can I help you?"

I went on. "Well, I want you to know that I just broke up a fight outside."

He encouraged me to share this with the school office, however, before I walked through the double doors, in my state of fury, Jesus spoke clearly to my heart. "So, YOU broke up a fight outside, did you? Did I tell you to get between two students and put your daughter and yourself in the middle of a fight?"

Of course, the answer was a solemn and embarrassing: no! I was quickly convicted with godly sorrow, by the Holy Spirit, and repented.

The Lord reminded me of the consequences of allowing festering frustration to take hold of my life instead of letting forgiveness inhabit my soul.

The anger I held toward my son's teacher had given me false confidence.

My self-reliance had placed my daughter and me in a potentially dangerous situation.

I knew the carnal feeling of boldness all too well, and it was not the Holy Spirit; it was my flesh rising up to take charge.

In my past, I had used anger to confront potentially uncomfortable situations instead of relying on the Lord.

The anger would motivate me to move past my tendency to be timid in situations where I needed gutsy courage.

The adrenaline flowing through my veins seemed to empower me to conquer any foe before me.

I failed to recognize the spiritual battle I was facing, attempting to fight with my carnal reaction, not responding to the Holy Spirit.

I was relieved and grateful the Lord had shown me my poor behavior because I am always eager to grow in my ability to walk in the spirit.

I went on to speak to my son's teacher.

Quietly and attentively, I sat and listened while she spoke using negative, hurtful, degrading words that enveloped the room.

The language she used showed me that she had lost her passion for teaching somewhere along her career path.

The negativity and disdain she displayed while talking about Jordan and her students was painful for me to hear. Unfortunately, her words and attitude reminded me of my father's.

My daughter and I left, and I was feeling uncomfortable, relieved, and a bit awkward.

I had never heard a teacher speak so offensively in my entire life, and she had no restraint when it came to expressing herself.

My heart was soothed, though, as I knew she was retiring soon.

Knowing the students in the upcoming years would not face her heavy hand, softened the picture I had formed in my mind of incoming students.

After returning home, I spoke to our son, reminding him we had to continue praying for her. She was obviously a hurting woman.

He hung in there like a champ and finished her class with a B. To God be all the glory.

Lesson #2

One morning, I was sitting on the bow of our lovely vessel, wearing shorts and a t-shirt sipping my coffee while moored in a harbor.

The sun cast its warmth over our day, inviting us to enjoy more moments of God's clear manifestation of heaven on earth.

The water is a special place my family regularly embraces. The memorable morning I am about to share was one that went down in the history of our remembrance. We often share this event with others because it is quite remarkable. While waking up, with caffeine in hand, I heard a woman screaming and shouting at the top of her voice, "Sh*t, sh*t, sh*t!"

I looked up and over to my right, where I saw a double-mast 55-foot sailboat coming directly at us – and it was not slowing down. I know it was 55-feet because the folks later let us know its size.

Our boat was a 45-foot powerboat – not small by any means, but not an enormous vessel, like the one barreling toward us.

The woman, screaming, was much older than I was. Her arms were extended as if to stop their boat from crashing into ours.

I quickly set down my coffee and with a burst of energy I leaped to my feet. I extended my arms toward the massive sailboat, and in a loud, bold voice, I said, "Jesus, Jesus, Jesus!"

Their boat came within a couple of inches of ours, and because it was so close, I did what any reasonable person would do; I grabbed their rail.

I pushed and pushed like the day I had delivered my baby, not wavering in faith, and obviously feeling overly confident.

It wasn't my finest moment, and I felt ridiculous after it was over. I had once again placed myself in a dangerous position and felt a bit sheepish.

Their boat did not collide with ours, and it was clear it wasn't me who had prevented it from doing so.

I messed up my back pretty bad that day and was humbled again after the Lord corrected me.

Again, he spoke clearly: "I did not tell you to touch their boat, Sherrie; I only instructed you to call out My name."

No need to touch a boat or break up a fight – just call on My Name, for all the power you need is in My Name Jesus!"

Lesson #3

Since I am a hairstylist, I visit the beauty supply store from time to time. I will be sharing a story of a morning when my daughter and I were out and about. She always loved going into stores, because she frequently talked me into getting her a little something.

After making a few stops, we ended up at our local beauty supply store, where professionals like me can purchase hair supplies for a reduced rate.

The store was across the street from a high school, and it was lunchtime.

After I completed my purchase, we exited the store and walked into the large parking lot, heading toward our vehicle.

I heard loud, screaming voices and also what sounded like slapping and grunts. Looking to my left, and saw a group of high school kids gathered in a circle, where a fistfight was taking place.

Horrified at what I was witnessing, I said to my daughter, "Honey, get in the car, quickly!"

She and I got in. Instantly, I locked the doors and got my cell phone out of my purse. With my phone in hand, dialing 911, I clearly heard the Lord say, "What are you doing?"

I said, "I'm calling 911, Lord."

God said, "Hang up the phone, go outside, and pray out loud."

Without hesitation, pushing aside my fear, I stepped out of my car, trembling. My heart was racing like a car in the Indy 500.

While standing behind my vehicle, about 50 feet from the fight, I pointed my trembling arm and finger toward the throng of teens.

The altercation was raging while I made my courageous stand. Suddenly, the Spirit of God and boldness rose from within!

It was as though I were alone on a mountaintop with a thousand angels, for I felt secure, much like Jericho's walls tightly closed up.

I prayed in my prayer language with sharpened volume, and my arm extended, I pointed toward the fight.

I carried a heightened expectancy to see God's authority put an end to this angry dispute.

The courage and boldness coming out of me was the Holy Spirit, I knew it with every fiber of my being. Within seconds, the fight broke up. The aggressive assembly of teens abruptly disbanded and walked away.

After returning to my car, the Lord spoke: "You see, Sherrie, there's no need to involve yourself by getting in the middle of things. When you call upon My name and pray, I will do what is not humanly possible and bring about a supernatural outcome."

I have consistently longed to live out my days on earth, displaying God's ability and not my own.

I want to be able to point to Jesus and give Him all the glory. That day, I was able to glorify His Holy name!

Zechariah 4:6 (NIV): "So he said to me, 'This is the word of the Lord to Zerubbabel:

'Not by might nor by power, but by my spirit, says the Lord Almighty!'"

Isaiah 41:10 (NIV): "So do not fear, for I am with you; do not be dismayed, for I am your God. I will strengthen you and help you; I will uphold you with my righteous right hand."

"Lord Jesus, as we search Your scriptures, we find many promises and life-imparting words.

The food You tell us to feast on, no longer in the natural, will surely sustain us as we journey through difficult times.

May Your secrets and mysteries, within our book of life's promises, be inscribed on the tablets of our hearts.

We are hemmed in, behind and before, shielded against the wickedness of the evil around us. As we are lowered into Your Well of living waters, submerged in Your ceaseless power, surely hope will mount up within our weary souls.

As Your strong arm lifts us out, we'll be launched into faith, escaping fatigue's relentless grip. Our requirements, penned within Your word, let us know to act justly, love mercy, and walk humbly with You.

Humility lifts us high, pride lays us low, and Your spirit leads us if we're stranded in sinking sand.

May You pluck us out of darkness and place us on Your immovable rock and fortress.

We'll stand unwavering in our faith, for we know that our help will continue to come rescue and redeem. Let us wave white flags of surrender throughout our days, Lord.

We will fly our flags high, signifying we have won the battle while surrendered to You, knowing the enemy is defeated." Amen.

Chapter 18

Another Giveaway!

While living in the area to which we had moved, we found God pulling our hearts toward another state.

We had family residing about five hours away and made the trek as often as possible. It was a twenty-four-hour drive when we lived in our home state; therefore, five-hours seemed like nothing.

After returning from one of our visits to AZ., my husband said, "If my boss gives permission to work virtually, perhaps we can move to AZ and buy a home."

We had a strong desire to purchase a home, instead of throwing our money toward an expensive rental.

We were excited about the possibility of purchasing a home with a pool

and the housing prices were super low at the time.

We prayed, relinquishing our will, letting the Lord know we wanted His.

Once again, we placed ourselves on the Potter's Wheel, ready to see God's plan unfold.

The next day, my husband let me know his boss was open to the idea. With this nod from his boss, and feeling the blessing from Jesus, we moved forward.

By the time we had moved away from our home state, with my hubby's permission, I had given away a large portion of our belongings.

With this next move coming up, I said, "Can we just give this all away? How can God give us more or different if we don't make room for it?"

He agreed, therefore, we gave away what we had not yet given.

Our couch, tables, pots, pans, dining set, and even our daughter's bunk bed were up for grabs.

I willingly released it all, giving it to many folks we knew who were in need. God's word says in Luke 6:38 "Give, and it shall be given, pressed down, shaken together and running over," so we decided to allow the Lord to fulfill that scripture.

Because we weren't able to find a place to buy right away, we decided to rent a fully furnished home.

After three months of looking for a home to purchase, we saw a house we both fell in love with.

Twelve months earlier, this home had been over $140,000 more than the current asking price.

It was 2010, and home prices plummeted because of the recession, so we had open doors to purchase this beautiful home. I asked our realtor, "Can you ask if they will leave us their couch, chair, dining table, pot rack, outside furniture, beds and dressers in the kid's bedroom, and the area rug?"

He said, "Oh, wow, sure. I will add those items to our offer."

They left us EVERYTHING we asked for—yes indeed, EVERYTHING! We were completely overwhelmed with joy and excitement at what God had done.

Over the years, we would sing songs in church, with the words in the chorus, "Open the floodgates of heaven, let it rain, let it rain." We honestly felt the blessing in what had taken place, and his supernatural reigning in our lives.

God reminded me of His word, "You have not, because you ask not."

I like to say, "It never hurts to ask the Lord for what is on our heart."

Many times it is the Lord who placed those desires within. When asking, I ask in humility and faith, for most of the time, the answer is yes. I believe God is good, and His goodness is just waiting to approach us, but it needs an invitation to do so.

Psalm 37:4 (NIV): "Take delight in the Lord, and he will give you the desires of your heart."

2 Corinthians 4:18 (NIV): "So we fix our eyes not on what is seen, but what is unseen, since what is seen is temporary, but what is unseen is eternal."

"Lord Jesus, all we have, and all we are, is because of Your great love and faithfulness toward us.

May we not disappoint, in the way we live our lives; wholly devoted to You, Jesus.

All we have is Yours, which includes our very lives. We trust in You, Lord, to usher in Your supply of our needs; knowing precisely what that is.

Let us lean into Your side, as You hold us tight, while we learn to place our hope in You.

Remind us, Lord, that You are extravagant and give us more than we need." Amen.

Chapter 19

Facing Goliaths With Faith!

Throughout our marriage, we've had the opportunity to pray for sick or terminally ill folks. God has had us pray over sick animals, plants, and even cars, which would not start. We would then watch God show up and show off His power.

We have witnessed dying pets healed, ailing plants live, and cars start after prayer when jumper cables did not work. I ran out of gas while in a small town at 10:00 PM, 45 minutes from my home.

There was no gas station in sight, and I did not have a cell phone; therefore, I called on the Name of the Lord.

"Lord, I know you can place fuel in my tank," I prayed, and I literally saw the gas gauge move up!

Before my eyes, He added one-quarter of a tank, and I made it home!

Another time, my costly glasses were lost while I was on a flight, after arriving back home from the trip. My husband and I searched and searched to no avail. The next morning, I said, "Lord, I want my glasses, please!"

God directed me to a small make-up bag in my purse, which we both had searched several times. There were my glasses, right ON TOP!

My husband lost his watch, which was an exceptional one. We prayed and searched everywhere but could not find it.

A month went by, and on a Sunday morning, while at church, I asked the Lord, "Show me where Steve's watch is, please." I saw a picture in my mind of where it was. When we returned home, I ran to our room and looked—and there it was, exactly where God said it would be. It was between the mattress and bed frame, resting in a corner.

My family has seen miracles come in all shapes and sizes. Over time, we have had to move briskly past the many naysayers who ridiculed our tenacious faith, unable to comprehend the idea that God cares about such things.

I have had the experience of watching God do the impossible, improbable, and illogical, therefore, I know, beyond a doubt, there is nothing God cannot do.

I'm often reminded of the story of David and Goliath.

David ran toward what armored soldiers were fleeing from when he showed up one day to deliver a measure of roasted grain and 10 loaves of bread for his brothers.

Little did he know he was there for something much bigger. David had no idea his life was about to be altered dramatically. His future would be set to a different course because of his unfaltering trust in God.

David ran *toward* Goliath while armored soldiers were retreating *from* him because he had confidence in God. He knew he had the backing of heaven.

He wasn't influenced by the size of the giant before him. No, he was more aware of the power of God than the size of Goliath.

Many of those present saw him as an arrogant kid with an issue called pride. David was a young man who was wholly devoted to God, investing his entire life in God's promises.

He was banking on God and given over to the One he knew would protect his future. David was overwhelmingly convinced God would never let him down.

He didn't let his mocking brothers, or the jeering soldiers, detour him from the reason he was there. Somewhere along the way, God derailed David's plan and placed His own upon David.

In my life, the Lord has instructed my husband and me to courageously move toward situations others refuse to enter. We are watchmen on the wall, keeping guard over the gates to our hearts.

We refuse to be intimidated by what we see if it appears impossible or risky.

The enemy must not gain a foothold to the entrance of our hearts, for his goal is to bring anxiety so that we will turn away from the Goliaths we are to face.

Many times, God has asked me to pray over a dying person, animal, plant, or car. I immediately have to take my thoughts captive and throw off the incapacitating fear attached to the negative words.

The biggest lie I have had to stand against is, "What happens if I pray and nothing happens?"

Pastor Bill Johnson said, "The most normal thing in the world is for a believer to have the appetite for the impossible. It is not normal, for a Christian, to not dream of impossibilities, bending their knee to the Name of Jesus."

You see, God longs for you and me to courageously run into places that others run from. This is where the impossible is birthed and where all things possible are brought forth.

2 Corinthians 10:5 (NIV): "We demolish arguments and every presumption that sets itself up against the knowledge of God, and we take captive every thought to make it obedient to Christ."

1 Samuel 17:45-47 (NIV): "David said to the Philistine, 'You come against me with sword and spear and javelin, but I come against you in the Name of the Lord Almighty, the God of the armies of Israel, whom you have defiled. This day the Lord will deliver you into my hands, and I'll strike you down and cut off your head. This very day I will give the carcasses of the Philistine army to the birds and wild animals, and the whole world will know that there is a God in Israel."

"All those gathered here will know it is not by sword or spear that the Lord saves; for the battle is the Lord's, and he will give all of you into our hands."

"Lord Jesus, may we attain this great faith, to believe You ARE the mountain Mover, gate Opener, way Maker, ground Taker, enemy Crusher, and Advocator; going before us and creating a way into our Promised Land. Once in our land, we'll plant flags of victory and remain steadfast in our authority to HOLD the ground we've been given.

May we be like David, who announced to the giant before him, just how things would play out.

David was not going to be intimidated; no, he was about to see history changed because of his unwavering faith in You Lord. Let it be the same with us, Jesus, for our course, is set before us by what we believe about You and what stands in our way.

We shall remember that praise and thanksgiving lead us in, and by Your grace, we shall abide while building our walls of remembrance. Lord, You are the Lifter of our heads, the Radiance of our faces, the Victor over our adversary, and the Restorer of all that was stolen." Amen.

Chapter 20

Ground Breaking
and Planting

My husband and I have had some difficult times in our 23 years when we've moved to different areas. Most folks may not move as frequently as we have; however, the Lord has had us on a different path, transplanting us much like a military family.

Since moving out of state, we've faced some new challenges, especially living in an area where many folks were of different religions.

Not everyone is eager to hear about Jesus; therefore, he and I share God's love and the many miracles He has provided. When we've trusted God with what we feel He wants us to say, He finishes what we began. He has shown us, He waters the seeds of faith we've planted in the hearts of those we share with.

There are times when it has felt as though we've had to use jackhammers to break through the religious cliques and walls we have encountered from folks in churches. We know the Lord wants us to be what is missing, and if friendliness is missing, we reach out to others and extend friendship to those who seem disquieted in their souls. We have willingly ventured out and cultivated the ground our prayers have broken through. God wants to use believers to share His love, and Steve and I are serious about heeding His instruction.

Whether it is a church, neighborhood, or place of employment, we've had to proactively reach out in the hopes of spreading God's love.

We have seen our acts of love and kindness melt hardened hearts and build relationships where there were none.

God reminded us we are to be bridge builders, taking people across the enormous crevasses of hesitation. Our experience is that typically folks are not comfortable being approached if there is no introduction.

Even when there is, maintaining a conversation can be grueling for some.

My experience as a hairdresser enabled me to navigate the uncomfortable first moments upon meeting new folks. It taught me ways to enter into the lives of strangers.

When I find myself in places where friendliness is absent, I know the Lord's assignment is to be friendly. If I perceive compassion or kindness is missing, then I am to be what is lacking, drawing from the Holy Spirit.

God has used my husband and me hundreds, if not thousands, of times to be what is absent in our churches or communities. I personally believe it is easier to sit back and observe when in a new setting, but God doesn't call me to be shy and withdrawn. Most often, the Lord has called me away from my comfort zone and beckoned me into a place where His power is needed.

God's will empower us to do what is necessary, to usher in Holy Spirit, which supernaturally imparts all that is needed; bringing in His presence.

My husband and I want to plant God's seeds of love and joy wherever we find ourselves. Hopefully, we will leave the ground we've taken for Jesus a little softer and more fertile for the seeds to grow in than the hardened ground we first visited.

Matthew 9:37 (NIV): "Then he said to his disciples, 'The harvest is plentiful; but the laborers are few.'"

2 Peter 3:9 (NIV): "The Lord is not slow in keeping his promises, as some know slowness. Instead he is patient with you, not wanting anyone to perish, but everyone to come to repentance."

"Lord Jesus, You long for us to bring Your Kingdom to earth as it is in heaven. May we be bold and courageous, not feeling fearful and weak, but empowered by Your great love toward us. We are not here for ourselves; we are here for You, Jesus.

Let us set aside our agenda and make room for You to change and transform us, while we enter and face situations we are not qualified for. We long to be Your hands, feet, and mouthpiece. Use us, Lord, for Your Glory!" Amen.

Chapter 21

Visions From His Kingdom Realm

One morning, I received what I'll refer to as a download from heaven. While making my bed, I had an impression of leg wear come to my mind.

Over the years, I've discovered I must not discount the seemingly random thoughts I may have. Too many vital revelations from God have come to me over the years. Any lack of my attention could cause me to miss what God has to say because it's often the Lord, broadcasting his plans and ideas. I want to be wholly dialed into the Holy Spirit and not miss one word He is speaking to me, because if I did, I might miss an opportunity.

This particular morning, I proceeded to take our beautiful multi-colored throw, which was lying across the end of our bed, and cover the lower portion of my leg. I remember thinking, 'This would make beautifully colored leg wear.'

At the time, I didn't know what kind of leg wear, or how to create them, but the thought and vision never left my mind or heart; and I held it near and dear. The impression followed me from our home state to our new one.

Within the first couple of months of our move, additional particulars of my husband's position were revealed, which included becoming a U.S. Patent Agent.

I remember pondering, when he told me what was required, "Mmmmm, I wonder what God is up to. Perhaps a patent on leg wear?"

Studying his heart out, night after night, after coming home from a busy day at work, was grueling for my husband. I watched him rise to the occasion each night, with not one single word of complaint.

The gigantic books, which looked like dictionaries, contained patent laws and all the detailed information pertinent to his patent test. "Most people don't pass the first time!" several people at work told him.

Well, *that* didn't instill the assurance he had hoped for. We knew the Lord had placed him where he was, and he held onto his confidence in God when he became weary from time to time.

It's interesting to me, the immense number of people who lean toward pessimism and who are often used to try and derail me from what God is calling me to do. Well-meaning folks who think they are realists, share their negative thoughts, but it doesn't sway me. I don't approach things with pessimism; because God has made me a dreamer, an innovator, and an optimistic person. Because faith expects and hopes, it is what I do.

Fast forward. My hubby did pass the patent test the first time he took it—glory to God! After a couple of weeks, we knew it was time for the vision the Lord had given me, for leg wear, to be brought forth.

I am not a seamstress, nor had I ever enjoyed sitting at a sewing machine; therefore, I knew this idea came from above.

I am a designer of hair, so drawing a pattern for this God-given leg wear was God's way of stretching me; it was not in my wheel-house. I inquired within my circle of friends, asking if anyone knew a seamstress who could help me lay out my idea on paper.

Sure enough, I was pointed in the direction of a woman who had the gift I was seeking. I sat and shared my vision for my leg wear, and we worked together to bring my idea to life.

She prayed with me, and a relationship developed between two lovers of Jesus. We worked together for a month, and finally, a pattern emerged. My husband began drawing the patent for Classy Calves. The small town where we lived had just opened a store that sold fabric PERFECT for my leg wear.

The seamstress made a couple of pairs, and they came out more astonishing than I could ever have imagined!

A few months down the road, the seamstress told me arthritis in her hands had flared up, and I would need to find another seamstress.

Thankfully, the Lord replaced her with another amazing seamstress—and of course, wouldn't you know it, she was a Christian as well. The Lord kept opening doors and gave me His favor at every turn. I often would chuckle at how God bestowed His great Grace, throughout our move of faith three years earlier.

Often, we didn't have to speak out our prayer for what we needed; He would fulfill our needs every time. Much like a waiter standing at a table, ready to chase down whatever is needed, all we did was think of our necessity, and it was met.

Very soon after things got rolling, the patent plans moved forward, and our family did as well, for we were called back to the state we formerly lived.

The Lord made it clear our time away had come to an end, and we needed to leave behind the many signs, wonders, and miracles God had done. We were about to enter an entirely new experience, which would test our faith and ability to trust God.

Unlike the ease I felt during our five-year trek away, we returned to relentless adversity, which kept coming at us, creating some truly dark times.

My dad had cancer, and it was serious. I was glad we were moving back home so I could be close to him.

Psalm 34:19 (NIV): "The righteous person may have many troubles, but the Lord delivers him from them all."

Habakkuk 2:2 (NIV): "Then the Lord replied: 'Write down the revelation and make it plain on tablets so that the herald may run with it.'"

John 20:21 (NIV): "Again Jesus said, 'Peace be with you! As the Father has sent me, I am sending you.'"

"Lord Jesus, we thank You for giving us a place to hide when fearful thoughts bombard our minds. With the helmet of salvation on, and our thoughts directed toward the Heavens, peace is assured. You call us away from the safety of the water's edge, where we can feel the sand beneath our feet.

Walking on water is only the beginning of the miraculous life to which you call us. Peering out to the tumultuous sea stirs fear, and believing we are to walk on top of it causes hesitation, and yet You petition us to come.

May we be a people who dare to face fear's ferocious roar, attempting to intimidate, holding us back from our destiny.

I pray that courage rises from within, and our spirit meets face to face with the enemy of our souls, and that we crush him with the weight of Your Glory. When we KNOW who we are, and to whom we belong, nothing will be impossible!

As boldness is heightened in our senses, may we be compelled to make a stand, for righteousness and justice, making way for Your Kingdom to come to earth." Amen.

"Willingly"
Book 2

by Sherrie Brown

Chapter 1

My Prophetic Dream

After we had lived away for five years, the Lord called us back home, where our journey had begun. God readied my heart before opening the doors to move again, taking us into another expedition, which held a tangible shift into a new chapter in the book of our lives.

Before returning, I had a prophetic dream, which ended up being a heads-up for us regarding the challenges that lay ahead.

In my dream, I was driving a Volkswagen Bug, similar to the one I'd owned as a teenager. I was quickly heading down a towering mountain in my car. Then I splashed into the ocean on impact and began to descend at an alarmingly sluggish rate.

My vehicle was utterly immersed as I traveled toward the bottom, encompassed by darkness.

Surprisingly, I was not frightened by the water and darkness rapidly pressing in. The speed I entered the water instantly slowed to a crawl, like a crab maneuvering along the seafloor.

As I traveled along the ocean's muddy ground, completely submerged and surrounded by water, it grew dim. It felt as though the murky waters of the deep were closing in on me. I finally took a moment and looked out my windows, and much to my surprise, I saw, through the dark waters, others had come in and were driving on both sides.

There were some on my left and some on my right. The expressions on their faces revealed their overwhelming anxiety and terror.

My first inclination was to stop and help! My compassion rose from within, and I felt compelled to cheer them on, however, I was fully involved with my own dilemma, and comforting them wasn't an option.

I experienced the pulsing, thrusting force, and the pressure of the sea that was terrorizing them. I was acutely aware of the intensity building around us, attempting to crush our cars, however, unlike the other travelers, I was wonderfully at peace.

One by one, as we all descended, entering increased darkness, other drivers began to take their hands off their steering wheels and their feet off their gas pedals. They were overcome, defeated by the waters of the deep. I was shocked to see they had given up, and I watched as they perished from their lack of perseverance.

Observing the heartbreak, seeing my fellow travelers lose hope and give up, I gripped the steering wheel tighter. I pressed on my gas pedal with supernatural strength and tenacity, feeling overpowered by the force of the Holy Spirit working within.

Much to my surprise, I didn't feel an increase in speed; however, I found myself delighted to be moving forward and making headway. Finally, I knew I had reached the end of my journey, as I could see the water becoming more transparent and brighter.

I began to ascend, climbing higher and higher, going faster until I finally burst out of the water and up the side of an enormous mountain—on the other side of where I had entered!

I began singing, shouting, and celebrating. I was overjoyed that I had survived. The journey up felt entirely different from my descent—literally throwing off the spirit of heaviness I had felt. I was now wearing garments of praise.

As my car moved forward, out of the seemingly endless journey on the ocean floor, it began to dry off from the water's of affliction. I then woke up.

Because the Lord had given me a word of life, I knew God had equipped me for the ride of my life that was coming through my prophetic dream. The word "through!" is one I embrace to this very day!

Whenever I read the word "through" in the scriptures, it means I can be confident that I have the victory!

Isaiah 43:2 (NIV): "When you pass through the waters, I will be with you; and when you pass through the rivers, they will not sweep over you. When you walk through the fires, you will not be burned; the flames will not set you ablaze."

Psalm 23:4 (NIV): "Even though I walk through the darkest valley, I will fear no evil, for you are with me; your rod and staff they comfort me."

Psalm 121:1-2 (NIV): "I will lift up my eyes to the mountains—where does my help come from? My help comes from the Lord, the Maker of heaven and earth."

Isaiah 55:12 (NIV): "You will go out in joy, and be led forth in peace; the mountains and the hills will burst into song before you, and all the trees of the field will clap their hands."

"Jesus, Your Kingdom has come upon us. Therefore, we are able to walk in Your dominion and authority. You showed me the scripture, Matthew (KJV) 17-21: 'Howbeit this kind goes not out, but by prayer and fasting.'

I believe, Lord, You cause the enemy to come out of hiding when we pray and fast. In the darkness and shadows, the enemy tries to hide, but Your matchless power causes our adversary to lose its place and surrender to You.

The enemies' camp, once having a secure place in our soul, is now exposed, and rendered POWERLESS!

Their influence over us was able to survive while living in darkness, but You, God, drove them out, and their demise is imminent! We proclaim, decree, and declare victory in our lives, allowing Your Light to shine in and through us.

The opposition that came at us is a springboard to our next level of Kingdom Power! From Glory to Glory, we will rise and ride on the Wings of Your Supremacy!

Keep us stealthy in the spirit as you take us in and bring us through to all You have prepared. Continue to give us Hinds feet, for Your high places, for we'll stand, proclaiming Your Name, Your Word, and Your Blood, watching mountains of impossibilities bow." Amen.

Chapter 2

Adversity Crashing In

Knowing we were moving back to our home state in 2013 brought me peace because I knew God had taken us by the hand and led us.

Often, when there is ease and a green light from God, my confidence dispels any fear or anxiety that could have arisen, as I know I had heard from Heaven's Throne.

I've experienced prophetic dreams for 30 years, and God shows me their meaning; however, this dream held many question marks, but I was confident God had equipped us.

Through this dream, the Lord spoke, "its time to buckle up, because you are about to embark on some heavy, burdensome times."

Unlike the faith bubble of 2008, when we departed, this was sure to hold challenges, and upon our arrival, we were hit.

Little did I know that our next season would feel more like being trapped inside a time machine, holding much darkness, with no place to disembark. I had mornings filled with despair and evenings with the same.

I was fighting the good fight of faith, which scripture talks of; however, it didn't "feel" good; it felt the opposite.

1 Timothy 6:12 (NIV): "Fight the good fight of faith. Take hold of the eternal life to which you were called when you made your good confession in the presence of many witnesses."

Psalm 42:11 (NIV): "Why soul, are you downcast? Why so disturbed within me? Put your hope in God, for I will yet praise Him, my Savior and my God."

"Lord Jesus, may our strength be renewed, like the wings of an eagle. Let us walk and not be tired or weary and run without growing weak. You have a plan for us, for a future, which is filled with hope.

I pray we do not lose our grip while hanging onto You and Your ability to carry us through every dark season we may encounter. As we rise in the morning, let our first thought be of You, the Lover of our souls.

With our thoughts on the Creator of our lives, full of love and compassion, dark days disappear and we are free to be elevated out of the dismal day in which we find ourselves.

Remind us how we begin our day has much to do with how it will come to a close. We choose to see Your smiling face throughout our day, feeling Your loving kindness and sensing Your very presence." Amen.

Chapter 3

In the Beginning

I was grateful my husband's company had paid our way, flying up to the state we had moved from and giving us time to find a home to purchase or rent.

The house we had left behind for the missionaries when we had moved five years previously was not available. We had new tenants, as the ministry people had moved on, and the new folks were locked into a lease; therefore, we sought to buy another residence. We had one week to find a home. It was not until after we arrived, our Realtor let us know she had only four days out of the seven to show us homes.

'Oh, boy!' I thought. 'We get to see what God wants for us, because, in my mind, four days to find a home is NOT enough time!'

We had learned from experience that there would never be a situation that would catch God off guard or surprise Him. We find when we remain hopeful; it eases stress and creates a sanctuary for us to abide in peace.

My husband and I have learned that God's provision will always be established and in place well before our need.

He is undoubtedly able and ready to save if the cards appear to be stacked against us. We searched with our Realtor and foraged through the Internet, looking for a home to purchase. We found nada, nothing, zip, zero.

My hubby and I created a list of all the things we wanted and a list of all we absolutely did not want.

Of all the homes we visited, not one of them fit the bill. We had to actively push back discouragement because we felt the pressure of the ticking clock.

Don't get me wrong, there *were* beautiful houses, but the home we longed for in our hearts and spirits had yet to be visited.

On the eve of the last day, we were able to view homes, I found, while searching the internet, what I believed was a perfect fit. I asked the Realtor if we could see it the next day, and she set it up.

She let me know it had not come up in her search, and she was surprised this home was up for sale.

After arriving, she let us know the owners had lowered the price by $40,000.00 one day earlier.

THIS was another miracle because we would not have qualified for the home if the price had been 40K more.

We walked through the house and were thrilled because our eyes were seeing everything we had hoped for in our hearts.

It was in a cul-de-sac, we had room to roam, and trees all around us.

Growing up with evergreen trees around me, I knew trees had to be part of the home's surroundings.

The Lord gave us more than we had asked for, and to this day, we pinch ourselves, as our home has been an enormous blessing.

Deuteronomy 1:11 (NIV): "May the Lord, the God of your ancestors, increase you a thousand-times, and bless you as he has promised!"

Isaiah 54:2-3 (NIV): "Enlarge the place of your tent, stretch your tent curtains wide, do not hold back; lengthen your cords, strengthen your stakes.

For your will spread out to the right and to the left; your descendants will dispossess nations and settle in their desolate cities."

"Lord, you know the desires within our hearts, because You are intentional in placing them there. I believe our steps are ordered by You, and when You created our destiny You were sure to include all of our dreams.

Lead us into our future, Lord, while we lean into You, finding ourselves joyful in heart because we have made You—and not what we have materially—our delight.

Thankful we are, and grateful we shall remain, while daily stepping into our pathway, leading to our forthcoming days, weeks, and years." Amen.

Chapter 4

Manifest Healing of My Heart

With the move back home, and while getting settled into our new life, my dad's deteriorating condition weighed heavily on my heart.

Watching my father go through the grueling process of cancer destroying his body was one of the most emotionally taxing events I'd ever lived through.

Thankfully, my relationship with my father had improved over the years. The healing of my soul, which God faithfully had completed, was evident.

Freedom and healing from the scars that my heart carried enabled me to enter into a right relationship with my dad, which displayed God's genuine love for him.

It is incredible what forgiveness can accomplish when we allow Jesus to mend. Embracing my freedom enables me to access my destiny, which seemed out of reach previously.

My dad, two years previous to cancer, had tearfully apologized to me.

He sat me down, and with tears, I had not previously seen nor words ever heard from his lips, he let me know he was sorry for his actions toward me.

My father passed away on Christmas, which was, for me, somewhat comforting.

I actually smiled when thinking, 'Isn't it just like You, Lord, to allow my dad to come to You on Christmas?'

He did not have a dramatic change in his irritable behavior. Still, I knew God was diligently working with my father.

I am confident I will see him again one day.

Psalm 23:3 (NIV): "He refreshes my soul. He guides me along the right paths for his name's sake."

Psalm 62:5 (NIV): "Yes, my soul finds rest in God; my hope comes from him."

"Lord Jesus, Your Word declares, when we forgive, we are forgiven. When we release forgiveness toward others, we are freed as well

We will access the blessings waiting to be poured out like a fountain of life. If we hold unforgiveness, its tight grip on us will hinder our ability to stand on Your Word and Rock.

We will quickly descend, sinking into dark and hopeless places, where prison bars are formed and freedom from Your Spirit is no longer felt.

The dismal shadows of despondency are not easy to exit, but when we forgive those who have hurt us, we are released into the fullness of our life in You.

Forgiving is a decision, one that imparts life and liberty to the one who once held the toxic poison of bitterness.

We choose to forgive, by faith, even if we have no feelings backing it. We'll assert our will and walk victoriously, freed from the enemies' lies, and remain in Your secret place Under Your Wings' Shadow."
Amen.

Chapter 5

Enter In, Go Through, Come Out Victorious

A couple of weeks after we moved into our new home, my husband was discarding wood, which the previous owner had left behind. A small board with a tiny nail broke in half, and the board flew up. The nail, which was protruding, penetrated his right eye.

The medics were called, and he was taken to the local trauma center. After a total of seven surgeries, six on his eye, including a cornea transplant, he was then able to see through the eye, which was injured within the first two years.

Our son, who was 22 years old at the time, was having health issues.

He had three back surgeries, one nose, a tonsillectomy, mono, and kidney stones, over the course of two years. He had a herniated disk from working out with Navy SEALs, and it needed surgery because of the nerve pain.

He was battling depression from all the trauma his body experienced and dealing with the pain.

My emotions were wearing thin, as the steady stream of what felt like waves of darkness continued its assault. Having to take care of my husband, son, and daughter, along with my father's health and my own back issues, caused my adrenal glands to fire and finally fizzle out. Fatigue settled in, and my energy level plummeted; I laid in bed for almost 3 months down for the count.

The town from which we had moved from had only two stoplights, therefore, having to drive in a major city with busy freeways was taking a toll on my nerves.

Being a *"taxi driver"* for my daughter, husband, and son, shuffling them to school events, hospitals for surgeries, and doctor appointments, had me reeling.

I was not able to step away from the fast pace of my days. My circumstances decided to govern my life, and there was no way to stop them.

I had experienced afflictions throughout the years, but I was able to face the trial with shining hope and endless courage during those times.

This time, it was as if someone had pulled my FAITH plug in the bathtub, filled with the water of trust and hope, which was quickly draining. There were moments of violent tugging on my soul as deep sorrow attempted to take me on an endless path of despair.

It brought back memories from my childhood when I was a little girl. Back then, when I saw water being sucked out of the bathtub, I would become frightened and panic.

This felt similar because I felt helpless watching my family plunging toward the drain of disappointment and destruction.

As an adult, I sensed the same fear was trying to permeate my entire body, pulling me back in time.

During previous attacks from the adversary, I clearly heard the Lord and could tangibly feel his presence; however, this time was unlike any other. Perhaps it was the mental and physical exhaustion overpowering me, stealing the peace I urgently needed.

God's loving nature was always my consistent anchor in times of difficulty.

For the first time as a believer, I was undergoing something *unique* and *iniquitous*. I was moving, ever so slowly through this period of affliction. The murky seawater of tribulation was much like my car traveling on the ocean's floor in my dream.

I continued to remind myself that God had given me provision for victory before I entered this distressing point in time.

Each time I felt defeated, I would spend time before the Lord, crying out in my anguish. As I did, I rose up in more power, feeling strengthened in my spirit.

Confidence began to bubble up as I made advancements for God's kingdom while using my shield of faith, avoiding all the darts of defeat coming toward me. I heard someone share, "Faith sees, hope feels, and love never fails."

God had given me five incredible years of miracles, on top of the 25 previous years of His endless love and power.

Because God had accomplished the impossible, those signs, wonders, and miracles laid a foundation which I could stand.

During our turbulent seasons, we learned the value of praising God while going through.

God does not want me to ask why he isn't coming to deliver me, but instead, He reminds me of His power working in and through me, enabling me to stand against the assaults of the evil one.

From what I have read throughout my years as a believer, *"Need does not move God; faith does."*

2 Corinthians 5:7 (NIV): "For we live by faith, not by sight."

Isaiah 40:29 (NIV): "He gives strength to the weary and increases the power of the weak."

2 Corinthians 4:8-9 (NIV): "We are hard pressed on every side, but not crushed; perplexed, but not in despair; persecuted, but not abandoned; struck down but not destroyed."

1 Timothy 6:12 (NIV): "We must fight the good fight of faith!"

"Lord Jesus, when we KNOW You, fear and anxiety have NO place to exist. Your PERFECT love, dwelling in us, creates a habitation to live in peace, and Your quiet calm longs to extend its roots within our soul, and make itself at home.

When we give fear a foot in the door to our hearts, fear will FIGHT to establish its place to abide.

Fear wants to rob us of our trust in You, Jesus. If we lose our trust and confidence in You, Lord, fear has won.

May we be diligent, actively pursuing You, with our entire hearts. You alone are worthy, Lord. You alone are to be praised!

Let us live with grateful hearts, and with thankful voices we will together celebrate our victory over our enemy called fear." Amen.

Chapter 6

Supernatural Favor and Healing

My husband continued to experience God's increase while he healed from *all* the surgeries and found a place to stand victorious during the increased spiritual warfare.

During this challenging time in which Steve found himself, he discovered more of the incredible nature of Jesus. Before this trial, my hubby had not seen evidence supporting God's supernatural ability to heal in his own life. He had seen the manifestation of God's power to miraculously heal others but had yet seen this in his own life.

He continued to make time to draw the design and write my leg wear patent. When dealing with the U.S. Patent Office, he knew he had to make sure all ducks were in a row. He had several of his own patents and was familiar with the required ins and outs. My original idea ended up becoming two unique designs, and we needed to submit them both.

During our conversations, the patent agent assigned to our case would say, "I'm not supposed to do this, but I will," or "I've never done this before, but I'll do it this time."

We had not asked for any favor; however, God's grace was standing watch over the process. We experienced access and acceleration in an endeavor many said would take many years. We encountered God's grace and favor all the way through.

From start to finish, the Lord opened wide the heavenly gates of His abundance, and we were granted two patents in a couple of years. We had been told by some folks, and were led to believe, it would take at least 10 years or more. We knew all along it would not take years for us, because we had memorials, written on our hearts of extraordinary tangible experiences of Gods favor over our lives.

I also received a patent on my trademark, "Classy Calves," along with two patents on my leg wear!

Ephesians 1:18-19 (NKJV): "The eyes of your understanding being enlightened that you may know what is the hope of His calling, what are the riches of the glory of His inheritance in the saints and what is the exceeding greatness of His power toward us who believe; according to the working of His mighty power."

Ephesians (NKJV) 3:20: "Now to Him who is able to do exceedingly, abundantly, above all we ask or think, according to the power which works in us."

"Lord Jesus, we truly live in the abundance of Your kingdom and Your love. Continue to lavish us with Your conquering love, causing us to be bulletproof and able to accomplish more than we ever would apart from You.

Remind us daily You have prepared our future, and as we walk daily on this earth, we will continue to see Your hand of provision for everything we encounter.

Thank You for going before us, Lord, creating ways when there appear to be none.

With You as our Rear Guard, we will experience Your unwavering commitment to secure us in our paths to the future of which we have been assured.

We will give thanks and praise while stepping into our destiny, one day at a time." Amen.

Chapter 7

She Fell and God Raised Her Up!

I brought my lead seamstress, to our home to help me in the interview process and hire a few capable seamstresses for my business.

One morning, while I was upstairs preparing for the day, I heard a loud bang and scream. I came down to see my friend on the floor, crying out in pain.

She had slipped and fallen, and her ankle felt broken. I immediately laid hands on her and prayed for God to heal her.

She hobbled into the emergency clinic near us, and the doctor on call said it appeared that her ankle was broken. However, they encouraged her to see her physician when she returned home three days later.

After returning home and seeing her physician, she called and let me know her doctor had taken more x-rays and declared, "Your ankle is not broken."

She said, "I absolutely know the Lord did a miracle the morning I fell!"

Every time I see God perform miracles, I just smile. God shows up, again and again, revealing His loving nature, and I can't stop grinning about the goodness of the Lord.

It is moments like these, I can feel hope increasing, and imparting faith, which is discernable and tangible.

Faith is the substance of things hoped for; therefore, I regularly remind myself to remain assured and full of hope in God.

My friends sometimes laugh because I genuinely expect all things will turn out well no matter what I see.

With absolute assurance, I believe God is faithful to bring about His plan, and when I know His plan has His goodness and not destruction, it's easy to trust Him with my life.

It is essential I know the nature of my loving Father and Savior.

If I have any part of me, think He is the author of death and destruction, how can I trust Him implicitly?

Psalm 34:19 (NIV): "The righteous person may have many troubles, but the Lord delivers him from them all, He protects all his bones, not one of them will be broken."

Psalms 107:20 (NIV): "He sent his word and healed them; he rescued them from the grave."

"Lord, our most significant achievements are conceived in the soil of our faith and determination.

The seeds we plant, watered by faith and hope, are brought to life when perseverance breathes on them.

May your Holy Spirit continue to ignite the fire within our souls and bring new life for us to be nourished and kept by You.

The food on which You want us to feast has nothing to do with our hunger pangs within our humanness, but with Your word daily feeding us, springing up to life now and eternal!" Amen.

Chapter 8

Pulling the Plug

While all this was going on, I found myself taking the advice my mentor had spoken 30 years earlier: "Take one day at a time."

I wanted to pull the supernatural electrical plug on the endless treadmill of cyclical tension.

One Sunday morning, my husband and I prayed specifically about stepping away from our leg wear company altogether.

During Sunday morning service, the pastor had the congregation walk up and take a scripture out of a box.

He said, "The scripture might be for you, or it might be for someone else." I remember thinking, I would give mine to someone else; however, after grabbing my scripture and reading it, I knew I would keep and embrace it.

God was speaking directly to me because it was a life-giving, hope-imparting word, which is still taped to my computer.

2 Chronicles 15:7 (NIV): "But as for you, be strong, do not give up, for your work will be rewarded," is what God had me choose from the God box that morning.

I cut back on the busy schedule I had created and learned a valuable lesson from the Lord.

It was evident that God was cultivating the soil of my soul, uprooting unhealthy patterns that did not benefit me.

God consistently releases His wisdom to live more freely, and in this time, I knew I needed to catch what He was teaching.

God was reminding me there would be seasons in life, it would feel like a carpet had been pulled out from under me.

The Lord spoke clearly to me, there will be situations which feel like your foundation was gone, but He was my solid Rock to stand on; no other surface is safe.

God said, "What seems like idleness, not knowing the direction you're business is going, is not you giving up."

I knew the Lord wanted me to quietly trust Him, and I so wanted to get this and have it saturate my very being. This season of seeming inactivity was, in fact, God imparting clarity and wisdom to my spirit.

I pay close attention to His voice, calling me toward something new.

I am determined to remain in a posture of waiting until it is clear God is waving me on, moving me ahead, right in step with Him.

I've learned to tarry, lingering longer than I had expected, abiding in a peaceful place, next to Jesus, not panicked but patient.

I have learned to live ready and willing and move ahead when He says move, standing still when He says to stand.

Isaiah 30:18 (AMPC): "And therefore the Lord (earnestly) waits (expecting, looking and longing) to be gracious to you; and therefore he lifts himself up, that he may have mercy on you and show loving-kindness to you. For the Lord is a God of justice.

Blessed (happy, fortunate, to be envied) are all those who (earnestly) wait for him, who expect and look and long for him (for his victory, his favor, his love, his peace, his joy, and his matchless, unbroken companionship)!"

"Lord Jesus, You declare, in repentance and rest, and with quiet trust is our strength. Your power, perfected in us, gives assurance we'll overcome all adversity. When the road seems dark, and the future looks dim, You broaden the path with Your light and love.

We see our red carpet of favor rolled out before us as we make our way to You. While showing us our glorious destiny, You point toward our journey ahead, giving a thumbs-up. You've asked, and not required, that we exercise our will as we make our way before You.

When we meet You face to face, we see acceptance in Your eyes, while being embraced by our Savior and Advocate. We cling to You Lord, enveloped by Your strength, leaning into Your deep compassion. As You wrap us tightly in garments of praise, we feel the heaviness we carried lift off.

May we continue to allow You to clear the road for our future and not try to create our own. We will learn to trust and release our lives into Your hands, abiding in Your great love and protection over our entire lives." Amen.

Chapter 9

Words to Live or Die By

Not long after I pulled the encouraging scripture from church, my father's health rapidly declined.

In the next few pages, I will be sharing a spiritual truth…but first, I'll provide a backdrop.

The truths I will share have powerfully influenced me, and I refer to them regularly while praying and sharing with others.

During one of my visits, my mother told me that she believed my dad had not heard his oncologist tell him at the last visit: the cancer was incurable, and he did not have much time left.

He had battled cancer before and survived, but this time, the doctor told him he wouldn't make it.

She said, "I am certain your dad didn't hear the doctor tell him he is not going to live."

She went on, "He isn't behaving like someone who just heard they are going to die. I know your father, and he would not be acting like this."

One time, while visiting, my 89-year-old father, he was replacing the flooring in their bathroom.

He was super cheery, laughing and upbeat, which was not his usual mood, and indeed not the attitude of someone who knew they don't have much time left.

I thought it was terrific that he didn't hear, for there was still a glimmer in his eye and a reflection of hope in his countenance.

My mom and dad didn't have a loving marriage; they were more like two siblings who held each other in disdain; quarreling throughout each day.

Walking through my own healing and deliverance gave me a closer look at my folks' relationship. I felt more equipped after seeing my folks' dysfunctional behavior to navigate the process of mending my heart.

The healing I carried caused the toxic words that had been spoken to me throughout my life to fall to the ground.

Over time, I did my best to forgive my folks, impart love, and demonstrate the character of Jesus.

There was clear evidence my soul was mended, when my father sat with me one evening with tears streaming down his face, and apologized.

He asked me to forgive him for his abusive behavior when I was young, which was monumental.

When I asked my dad if I could pray for him throughout the years, he never once turned me down.

In fact, he was more than open to hearing about Jesus as time went on.

The sparkle in my dad's eyes, which I witnessed during my last visit before he died, reflected the restoration between my father and me.

A couple of weeks after we visited my parents' home, my dad and mom went back to the doctor. This time, my mom made SURE my father heard the doctor say, "You won't make it this time because cancer has spread!"

After hearing those words, my father's health declined rapidly. He went to be with Jesus a few days later, on Christmas.

He heard the words of a mere man, which greatly affected him because he did not know, nor understand Jesus gave us the power to stand against them.

I have had many occasions when a physician has given me a frightening diagnosis, and I stand against the prognosis.

These experiences have taught me how to exercise my faith and push back the fear attached to the words any doctor speaks.

I am cordial if a Dr. tells me upsetting news.

I listen and then simply let them know I'm grateful for their time and leave the office without their words attached to me or my future.

I believe it matters how I receive what I hear from a doctor.

It has been vital that I not align myself with their words as fact and final.

I feel blessed knowing my dad is in heaven, even though he suffered horrific pain through cancer.

Yes, his life ended, and cancer killed him, but Jesus has him, and he is whole and healed! For this, I celebrate!

Hebrew 11:1 (NIV): "Now faith is confidence in what we hope for will actually happen; it gives us assurance about things we cannot see."

John 10:10 (NIV): "The thief, satan, comes only to kill, steal, and destroy; I came that they may have life, and have it abundantly."

"Lord, You are the Word, and we must remember to declare Your power-filled words daily. We long to be your instruments, bringing forth heavenly sounds and music to Your ears.

As we begin our day, may we speak Your life-giving, life-changing words, and watch our environment change. You fill the atmosphere as we release our testimonies into the earth. As we walk in Your anointing, the spiritual climate changes, and we usher in Your presence and glory. May we not take lightly the charge you've given us to go out and heal the sick, cleanse the leper, cast out demons, and usher in Your glory!" Amen.

Chapter 10

What's That You Say?

I am going to share a couple of key lessons my husband and I deem spiritually valuable. I hope you find them to be of value as well.

Lesson #1 When my dad didn't "hear" the doctor tell him that he didn't have much time left, he indeed wasn't affected.

It wasn't until he *actually heard* the news from the doctor, foretelling his future that he declined rapidly.

Even if I listen to a physician sharing the prognosis of death, I do not have to receive the doctor's words into my spirit, as my fate, fact, or final.

It was not until my father "heard and received" the oncologist's information that he rapidly declined.

Suppose a doctor lets me know his diagnosis or prognosis, telling me I have an incurable disease. It likely will cause a tremendous amount of anxiety and an opening to impact my body, mind, and spirit.

I've had fear hit me like a locomotive, causing my heart to skip quite a few beats.

As I shared previously, throughout the years, I have tangible experiences, where God has miraculously shown up, which has helped to diminish fears attacks.

Because God has consistently delivered me from all of my fears and troubles, I walk in more confidence.

The Lord has held firm to His principles and flawless word, and He backs up His Name implicitly.

God is Holy, and His Holiness is His beauty and His wonder. Holiness is the representation of His nature and presence on earth. He implores us to be holy as He is Holy. He also lets us know the pure in heart shall see Him.

I genuinely believe we who choose purity not only see Him, but we feel and hear Him more clearly as well.

When we undoubtedly hear the voice of our Savior, we can then expose the lies of our enemy.

Knowing that fear is a liar will stop the assaults on our mind and body, allowing us to walk in liberty, free from the ongoing attacks.

1 Peter 1:15-16 (NIV): But just as he who called you is holy, so be holy in all you do; for it is written: "Be holy, because I am holy."

Psalm 16:8 (NIV): "I keep my eyes always on the Lord. With him at my right hand, I will not be shaken."

Psalm 107:19-20 (NIV): "Then they cried to the Lord in their trouble and he saved them from their distress. He sent out his word and healed them; he rescued them from the grave."

God's word is packed with scriptures, letting us know the Lord saves, delivers, and heals, as well as restores and creates, taking us in and bringing us out, and on to victory.

We read in Job about how fear can impact the outcome of a trial.

Job 3:25 (NIV): "What I feared has come upon me; what I dreaded has happened to me."

Often, what we expect, prepare for, and predict will actually come to us because this is what we are equipping ourselves for.

I heard someone say, "Faith is believing what we cannot see will come to pass, and fear is believing what we cannot see will come to pass."

I appreciate physicians and always have; I'm certainly not saying I am against them.

Friends, I wholeheartedly believe if the message I am listening to in my mind, brings fear, the messenger is not God.

I must take my thoughts captive, even if it is over and over each and every day!

God sent His word to heal and deliver us out of pits. He doesn't deliver and throw us into them.

Two timeless quotes come to mind: "Sticks and stones can break my bones, but words can never hurt me," and "What you don't know won't hurt you." Because I had to spend years coming out from living under the toxic words spoken over me as a kid, I am all too familiar with how words influence.

Yes, words do inflict pain and cause many injuries to our souls! Being called a loser, stupid, and a quitter took its toll on my life before I received Jesus.

Those devastating and influential words did not have a hold on me after Jesus set me free, and I am forever grateful.

The second quote is impactful, as well. Therefore, I want to apply God's word to every situation in my life, not letting negative words come over me like a spell.

What my dad didn't know did not affect him, but then he heard the physicians words, and those words took him in a direction, different from the one he was on.

God's word has taken me, time and again, in the right direction; God Kingdom path!

Romans 8:28 (NIV): "And we know that in all things God works for the good of those who love him, who have been called according to his purpose."

Jeremiah 29:11 (NIV): "'For I know the plans I have for you,' declares the Lord, 'Plans to prosper you and not to harm you, plans to give you hope and a future.'"

If a physician, or any person who has authority in my life, brings grim or frightening information which knocks me back on my heels and takes my breath away, it's best to not embrace and receive the information as fact and final.

Lesson #2 Through His word, God shows us that He has life, liberty, and freedom in the Holy Spirit.

The Scriptures impart life and hope, and if someone is sick and needs healing, God say's to pray and believe, and they can and will be healed.

I have personally seen Jesus heal people—even my own husband, daughter, son, and myself, when the prognosis was grim, even unto death.

Friends, the reason I emphatically refuse to embrace bad news is that I have story after story of God turning awful news to good news.

I respectfully listen to what a specialist says and then let it be *information*, showing me precisely *how* to pray.

Psalm 107:20 (NIV): "He sent out His word and healed them; He rescued them from the grave."

Isaiah 53:5 (NIV): "and by His stripes, you are healed."

Proverbs 18:21 (NIV): "The tongue can bring death or life; those who love to talk will reap the consequences."

Proverbs 21:23 (NIV): "Those who guard their mouths and their tongues keep themselves from calamity."

James 3:6 (NIV): "The tongue also is a fire, a world of evil among the parts of the body. It corrupts the whole body, sets the whole COURSE of one's life on fire, and is itself set on fire by hell."

1 Corinthians 10:10 (NIV): "And don't grumble as some of them did, and then were destroyed by the angel of death."

Proverbs 4:23 (NIV): "Guard your heart above all else, for it is the source of life."

Hebrews 10:23 (NIV): "We must hold fast to the confession of our hope, unwavering; for He who promised is faithful."

"Lord, Our words are affected by the condition of our heart. May the words we speak be FULL of Your life and power. I pray we will examine ourselves daily, allowing You, Lord, to heal our hearts and tongues. Forgive us for speaking destruction and death, and not life and hope.

Lead us to Your Living Water and Word, which heals our hearts, for our lips to speak praises to You!

Forgive us for opening our mouths with words of frustration and not speaking forth Your life-filled May what we speak, create a world for us to live in, and bring Your Kingdom Canopy to cover us.

Cleanse and heal us, oh Lord. We long to lift You up and express our thankfulness with our praises and not complaints. Take us, shake us, sift us and prune us. We long to resemble You Lord, courageous and bold, willing to stand up and fulfill Your purpose in our lives" Amen.

Chapter 11

I'm a Living Testimony!

As you have read, over the years, I've learned the importance of embracing God's word over what a doctor might say.

My OB/GYN told me, years ago, "It is more than likely you'll not be able to conceive."

The surgeon made this declaration after my left ovary and tube were removed at age 20 because of endometriosis.

Endometriosis is a disease in women, which often causes sterility.

It can also have life-threatening complications, and at times goes on undetected, which was the case with me.

Today, I am thrilled to say I have two children, ages 29 and 17.

My orthopedic surgeon told me when I was 21, "You will never have a full range of motion in your leg, and you most likely will be using a cane throughout your life."

I had torn my A.C.L. (Anterior Cruciate Ligament) when I was 20 when I was dirt biking and really done a number on my knee. I tore it up, and it wasn't a simple fix. I used to be quite the tomboy when I was young.

Since then, I have never had an issue with my knee, and I have been water-skiing, mountain skiing, and playing many sports, along with routinely exercising.

I've not needed a cane or any kind of leg brace.

On two different occasions, I was also told, "There is a chance you have breast cancer."

The specialist based their remarks on what was found during a routine mammogram.

Both times, upon further testing, nothing was found.

In 1999 my husband had a reverse vasectomy after much prayer and discussion about having another baby. He was told to hurry if we wanted to conceive, as they tend to close up quickly.

Previous to his decision to have surgery, I had visited three doctors over three years. I was told I had little to no chance of conceiving at my age.

They said, "You have no left ovary or tube, you had endometrioses, you're at the end of menopause, and you are 40 years old. Sorry, but it is highly unlikely you will have another child. I conceived my daughter at the age of 44.

During a visit to the hospital to have an ultrasound performed, when pregnant with my daughter the technician was having a difficult time finding my baby's size.

Since I had an incredible amount of amniotic fluid, we were sent to this specialist to find her exact size. Within the first minute, the Doctor said to my husband and me, "I am so sorry, I am so very sorry." Right then, my heart stopped, then pounded so hard I could barely concentrate.

He pointed to the ultrasound screen, showing us the base of our baby's skull.

He said, while his hand was on the screen, "Her skull has a large opening at its base, and with the amount of amniotic fluid you have, the pressure will damage her brain.

He said, "You will need genetic counseling to prepare yourself for a disabled baby."

Initially, fear hit me like a Mack truck, but all at once, the Spirit of the living God rose up, and I declared, with a smile and faith-filled words, "Thank you, Doctor, for sharing. Now we know how to pray."

I went on, "You see, Doctor, I don't have a left ovary or tube because I had endometriosis. The surgeon removed both. Also, I am 44 years old, and my husband had a reverse vasectomy four years ago. Our baby is a miracle, and we are certain she will be perfect."

He was surprised and said, "You're 44? I will pray, too!"

Our daughter was born four months later, perfect!

In fact, she has been in accelerated classes and on the honor roll since fourth-grade. She is now a senior in high school, attending A.P. and honors classes with a 4.0-grade point average.

As I have repeatedly shared, I am not against doctors. I believe they are gifted and much needed.

However, I've learned to place more faith and hope in God's Word and His consistent integrity, displaying His miracle-working power.

In my opinion, I believe doctors are called practitioners because they are still *practicing*.

God is *not* practicing. His word is flawless, and by His power, completely able to perform to perfection – everything pertaining to my life and hope for my future.

I've received bad news over the years, from doctors, attorneys, and meteorologists. Each time bad news is given, I don't accept it. I hold up God's word and begin to declare it as truth over me.

2 Corinthians 10:5 (ESV): "We destroy arguments and every lofty opinion raised against the knowledge of God, and take every thought captive to obey Christ."

I know God's will is for me to have a full and abundant life and also know I have an enemy who wants to steal it; therefore, I must actively fight to attain and keep it!

John 10:10 (NLT): "The thief comes only to steal and kill and destroy. My purpose is to give them a rich and satisfying life."

Time and again, my prayers were answered; for better health when I wasn't well, for provision when I had none and restoration in every area of my life.

Over the years, we have scheduled days for using our boat for ministry, and rain was predicted.

With diligence, we prayed for sunshine when rain and strong winds were predicted, and God answered, giving us awesome weather.

We woke up to rain, wind, and white caps one day when we were scheduled to have ministry time. I grabbed Steve's hand and we walked out to the boats bow, declared the winds and rain to cease, and watched God literally calm the storm!

One Saturday evening in December, we scheduled a gathering of co-workers and friends on our 46-foot Chris Craft for the Christmas parade of boats.

When extending the invite, my husband told folks, "If it is raining, we won't be going."

On the day of the parade, the rain was heavy, and the winds were blowing, which is not fun when one is out on the water.

I heard my husband answer the phone and tell the person on the other end, "Yes, it's canceled. We won't be taking the boat out in this rainy weather."

After he hung up, I declared, "WAIT...WHY did you cancel? Call them back. We are not going to cancel, because the rain will stop. We've prayed, and I believe the rain will cease."

I reminded my hubby, when we pray the prayers that Jesus prayed, even over the weather, we are told He will answer!

My husband called back the person, letting them know we were still on. About three hours later, we headed to the boat in the pouring rain.

As we drove south down the interstate, the rain ended, and the night became unseasonably warm. There was no sign there was any rain; skies were clear. The water was also extraordinarily calm, which reminded us of God's power to make possible what some deemed impossible.

Everyone showed up that night, and everyone enjoyed the Christmas festivities.

At one point, we heard over the V.H.F. radio, the captain of the parade's lead boat. He announced, "I've never seen such nice weather in the 20 years I have been doing this." We were grinning from ear to ear, as we knew without a doubt, our faith cleared the way for a perfect evening.

As the night ended and we pulled our boat back into her covered moorage, it began to rain.

My husband called everyone to attention and shared with the folks that he hadn't had faith that the rain would stop. He let them know he had to repent for having no faith, and it was only at my insistence, we kept our plans and didn't cancel.

It was a teaching moment, and we were able to share our story of faith with all who attended.

God has reminded us we have not because we don't ask, often thinking God isn't interested in things like the weather.

We say, "Yes, He is!"

John 16:24 (NIV): "Until now you have not asked for anything in My Name. Ask and you will receive and your joy will be complete."

Mark 4:39 (NIV): "He got up, rebuked the wind and said to the waves, 'Quiet! Be still!' Then the wind died down, and it was completely calm."

James 5:15 (NIV): "And the prayer offered in faith will make the sick person well; the Lord will raise them up. If they have sinned, they will be forgiven."

John 14:12 (NIV): "Very truly I tell you, whoever believes in me will do the work I have been doing, and they will do even greater things than these because I am going to the Father."

I was, and am still, mentored by folks who have a ministry of seeing God do the miraculous.

I read in God's words that we have all been called by the very One who died for us, to display the mighty works of His kingdom.

When I first gave my life to Jesus, I chose to put my trust, faith, and hope in Him.

He is noble and trustworthy, with flawless character, and I place myself in His care daily.

I have never been disappointed or let down by Him, for He indeed is reliable and noble, deserving of all my praise!

God works all things together for His glory and our good. If something does not look good, He is not finished.

I believe my expectations of Jesus answering my prayer bring more answered prayers into my life.

If I agree with the weather forecasters, those very forecasters hold my future plans.

To this day, if we see rain in the forecast and have an event scheduled, we pray over the specific day, or days, for the weather to be perfect. Ninety-nine percent of the time, it is.

God loves to smile over us, and often He shows His exceeding joy by answering prayer regarding the simple things, simple to Him, not to us.

Philippians' 4:4 (ESV): "Rejoice in the Lord; again I will say rejoice."

Romans 15:13 (ESV): "May the God of hope fill you with all joy and peace in believing, so that by the power of the Holy Spirit you may abound in hope."

"Lord Jesus, we thank You, for You make a way if there appears to be none.

You open doors and bring us favor if we are facing closed doors. You close doors, often preventing us from venturing out where we don't belong.

I pray we dare to ask that our joy may be full. We are Your delight, and You are ours.

Often, we have not because we do not ask; therefore, I dare to ask for what looks to be impossible, because You love to rock our world with answered prayers.

The king asked Queen Esther, (NIV) 5:3: 'What is it Queen Esther? What is your request? Even to half the kingdom, it will be given you.'

You let us know, throughout Your word, that the Kingdom of God is available to us; yes, even ALL of Your Kingdom can be ours.

We embrace Your word, Lord, and hold fast to it, releasing Your word accompanied by our faith to the world around us. May we represent You and Your Kingdom well, Lord. I pray You find us as doers of Your word and not only hearers!" Amen.

Chapter 12

Raising the Victory Flag

One of the most valuable lessons I have personally learned in all my years with Jesus is this:

"I must be flexible, with an open heart and ears, to hear the Lord's instructions.

My hubby and I want to be obedient to God's call.

We want to respond immediately, and follow where He's leading if He says the time is now."

Many of you know the story of Peter and Andrew. Jesus saw them as they were casting their nets into the lake because they were fishermen. Matthew 4:19-20 (NIV): "Come follow me," Jesus said, "and I will send you out to fish for people." At once, they left their nets and followed Him.

When we have let the Lord know He is free to do His will in our lives, He knocks our socks off—which we've found He LOVES to do!

The Lord placed our son on our hearts during prayer one morning because he had many physical and emotional battles.

Within three years, he had four surgeries, kidney stones, and mono. We knew the Lord would be the only One who could advance our son and launch him into his path of healing and wholeness.

During our worship and prayer time, we heard the Lord call us to buy a home to use as rental property.

God let us know this would enable our son to move out and on, opening new doors and opportunities for his future.

We were not thinking about buying any rental property. We had learned this was typically a sign that we had heard correctly; because it was not on our radar whatsoever.

Often, this was how we knew we had indeed heard from the Lord because the words and ideas would "come from left field" during prayer.

This particular morning, after our prayer, I headed out for the day. I was driving through our neighborhood when I saw a "For Sale" sign.

It was on a house two blocks from ours, which I drove past from time to time and had not seen until that very day.

I called the agent's number and asked if it was available. She quickly answered, saying, "Yes, it is still for sale. It is a short sale and has been on the market for almost three years, and the price was reduced $40,000 yesterday."

I got a hold of my husband right away and then called our friend, who was a Realtor.

He came over later that day, and we were able to see the inside of the house.

We could not believe how lovely it was! It looked as though the previous owners had rarely lived there.

After having sat for so many years, the yard was pretty shabby, but the inside only needed some paint and deep cleaning.

We came back to our house with our Realtor, and were super excited about moving forward.

He let us know it would most likely be a lengthy process if we proceeded, perhaps dragging on for a year or two because there were two banks, and it was a short sale.

He also declared, "There will be a charge from the water district, which will need to be paid upfront. The cost to you will be $1,200.00."

He explained, "The water-sewer company gives a courtesy turn on for inspections, but you will also need the water on for the appraisal.

My hubby said, "We are NOT going to pay that!"

Our friend said the owners had not paid the water-sewer bill for three years, hence the high bill.

My husband replied, "I guess we will call it off, then."

I boldly spoke up: "WAIT! Can we please pray and see what God wants to do? Let's allow God to show up. From my experience, these are the kinds of situations that God loves to involve himself in."

I asked them to let me pray in the morning, and then speak to the water department. They agreed, and the next day, after prayer, I went to the water department and talked to their billing person.

She looked up the account on the house we wanted to purchase and said, "Actually, no, there is no $1,200 charge. It is only $45.00."

I am standing there, not shocked in the least. This was another arrow in my quiver, my arsenal of testimonies of God's greatness!

Leaving with a massive smile on my face, and could not wait to share the news with my husband and Realtor friend.

After letting them know the fantastic news, our Realtor was stunned, since he had been told it would cost $1,200.

He recognized, right away, it was the Lord, and we moved forward with our purchase.

The inspection showed that the siding on the home was rotten, therefore the entire house needed new siding.

I called a few places and put together a list of bids. We chose a reputable contractor who was asking approximately $20,000 for all the work needed.

My husband called our Realtor and said, "Let's ask if the banks will take $20,000 off the asking price."

Our Realtor announced, "There is absolutely no way you will get two banks to agree on lowering the price in this booming housing market after they just reduced the price by $40,000."

Once again, with confidence in God, I declared, "Let's see what God wants to do! We need to move ahead and ask both banks if they will lower the price to reflect the needed work."

A few days later, we heard back from him, letting us know God had answered our prayers. The two banks did agree to lower the price by an additional $20,000 to cover the cost of new siding and paint!

Again and again, the Lord showed up, and we were able to honor Him with thankful hearts!

Isaiah 55:9 (NIV) "As the heavens are higher than the earth, so are My ways higher than your ways and my thoughts than yours."

Our Realtor friend kept scratching his head along with praising God, recognizing this was the Lord's hand.

The house closed the end of April 2016, and our son moved in shortly after.

Within two months of living there, his life began to turn around because he had stepped into his God-ordained destiny.

He found a friend to rent one of the rooms, and we sought out two other tenants to rent the remaining two.

Our son was divinely launched into his future, where God's blessings and anointing lay waiting.

This new place held hope and promises from the Lord he had not experienced previously.

Within the first two months, our son attained an excellent job and met a young lady. Within the year, he proposed.

They married in 2017 and are both doing well, currently expecting their second child.

God opened the doors every step of the way and gave us His favor.

I said to my husband, "How can I say I have faith in God if I am not willing to be placed in front of situations where I actually need Him?

My sincere desire is to consistently acknowledge God, the One who brings about miraculous outcomes when I step out of the way.

I love giving Jesus full access to my life because I know that He has the very best for me in mind.

Corrie ten Boom writes: "Faith sees the invisible, believes the unbelievable, and receives the impossible."

Matthew 7:7 (NIV): "Keep on asking, and you will receive what you ask for. Keep on seeking, and you will find. Keep on knocking, and the door will be opened to you."

Mark 11:24 (NIV): "Therefore I tell you, whatever you ask for in prayer, believe that you have received and it, and it will be yours."

Matthew 17:20 (N IV): He replied, "Because you have so little faith. Truly I tell you, if you have the faith as small as mustard seed, you can say to this mountain, 'Move from here to there.' And it will move. Nothing will be impossible for you."

"Lord, when You come knocking at our door, I pray faith answers and not fear or doubt. May we open wide our hearts and souls to You, allowing You passage, that we would enter into all heaven holds for us.

Trustworthy is Who You are, and faithful is who we long to be. No longer will we be sitting in the boat of doubt, with a sea of confusion tossing us to and fro.

We will feel Your peace released in our souls as we bow and give entrance to Your loving-kindness. You have what heaven holds, which longs to be established in our lives. We say, 'Yes Lord, YES! Welcome in and never leave, for I trust in You!'" Amen.

Chapter 13

No Grumbling, KNOW God's Blessings

In May 2017, we decided to have the windows replaced in our 28-year-old home. The seals were broken, and the condensation on the windows made it impossible to see through them.

Also, we could practically watch the heat depart through the windows during the winter months. Our electricity bill in the winter was horrible.

There were many companies from which to choose, but we ended up hiring a smaller one because of its price point and excellent reviews.

The windows we chose were going to have an enormous impact on our winter heating bills and summer air conditioning bills. We were also super excited at the thought of being able to see through our windows.

The window installers were super polite and kept everything protected during the entire process. It only took only three days.

Once the work was done, my husband noticed the windows on the lower portion of our home, which were supposed to have special tint, did not have it.

I called the owner of the company, who had written our initial order, and let him know about our discovery. He was speechless and apologetic, asking what he could do to make things right.

My hubby and I talked and prayed about how to handle the mistake. We moved forward, letting him know we would leave them as they were, and move on.

I am sure he was shocked because most folks would most likely have complained and wanted them replaced with the correct ones.

They were gorgeous, and the lack of tint did not make much of a difference.

Truthfully, we didn't mind the mistake, as the new windows were beautiful.

We let the window company owner know we were perfectly happy with the windows installed, even though we didn't have the tint we had desired.

I wrote an outstanding review on Yelp because our experience had been fantastic.

We believe what we sow we reap. I do not like to complain about service in a restaurant or business, not meeting our expectations.

I imagine myself in certain situations, having owned my own business over for the last 40 years, and know mistakes can and will be made.

Unless it is a life-altering situation, we extend God's grace and let things slide.

There are a couple of takeaways, along with a tremendous blessing, in the entire situation.

The owner did not ask for the remaining $7,000 due when the job was finished.

Perhaps if we had thrown a fit and demanded they take out the windows, or wrote a horrible review on Yelp, the entire scenario would have ended dramatically differently.

I am not saying it's appropriate to give in if a company, or person, doesn't perform their job correctly or installs sub-par items.

On the contrary—had they done a poor job, or if the windows had not been similar to what we had ordered, we would have spoken up.

We did not feel the Lord gave us the nod to complain about five windows that did not have tint. Instead, we had peace regarding our situation and felt content.

These folks knew we were Christians. My husband and I believe it is essential while navigating through life, to make sure we leave behind a good impression—one that points to God.

James 3:17 (NIV): "But the wisdom from above is first of all pure. It is also peace loving, gentle at all times, and willing to yield to others. It is full of mercy and good deeds. It shows no favoritism and is always sincere."

Hosea 10:12 (NIV): "Sow righteousness for yourselves, reap the fruit of unfailing love, and break up your unplowed ground; for it is time to seek the Lord, until He comes and showers His righteousness on you."

"Lord Jesus, I truly believe if I resist being critical, and instead pursue gratitude and thankfulness, I will reap those attributes.

What I sow, whether it be encouragement and praise, or complaining and criticizing, I will bring toward me what I release.

Lord, we choose to release hope, faith, and love, and as we do, we will be certain to live in the blessings held within them. Continue to teach and correct us, Lord, for we long to be transformed into Your likeness.

We will not stop seeking Your love and mercy, Lord.

You remind us, in Your word, we shall see Your goodness, along with the constant protection You provide as we discover more of You.

Hide us, keep us, and point us toward the way, where our path is straight and leads to Your Throne of Grace." Amen.

Chapter 14

I Know the Plans for You

One morning, before we prayed, I said to my hubby, "You have been speaking quite a bit about retiring. How about we pray and ask God what he wants you to do?"

We asked God to reveal His will pertaining for Steve's retirement, and shortly after, he left for work.

About two hours later, my phone rang. "Well, I guess God doesn't want me to retire," he said. "I just got a promotion and raise!"

I laughed, covered in what I call "Holy Ghost Goosebumps," and replied, "Boy, that was a quick answer!"

Frequently, during prayer, we expose our hearts to the Lord, agreeing with Haggai 2:9 (NLT): "The future glory of this Temple will be greater than its past glory, says the Lord of Heavens Armies, and in this place, I will bring peace. I, the Lord of Heavens Armies, have spoken."

Steve and I desire to accomplish all God has for us, defeating the darkness and ushering in His love and presence.

The Lord knew we had wished for our latter years to apprehend and hold more than our former ones.

We often discuss ways to ensure we finish our lives in a way that displays God's love and glory.

I've journeyed through enough seasons to know God's increase is attainable when I relinquish my entire life to Him.

I let Him grip me tight and hold me securely, allowing His wondrous Kingdom power, to enter my world.

He overcame the world for me to overcome my own by relinquishing my will to Him.

His power is perfected in my submission and surrender to my merciful Savior.

A couple of months later, during our prayer time, I received a vision and prophetic word for my husband.

I saw Steve in a meeting at the corporation where he was employed.

He was sitting in a circle with his peers.

His co-workers were arguing, raising their voices in a heated debate.

My husband stood up, and boldly asked, "Are you all done shouting and arguing?"

With all eyes on him, he walked over to a closet door, opened it, and pulled out a cannon.

I began sharing with him what God had shown me about the upcoming events in his future, making their way into his current life.

Because prophecy is foretelling and forth telling the future, God was clearly letting him know He was about to embark on a wonderfully new and exciting season.

God was letting my husband know his plans for the future and his new role. The Lord would be strategically placing him within the company, and he was excited to watch it all unfold.

My husband was about to have a powerfully impact within the group he led and would be used dynamically to bring about a much-needed shift.

The anointing of God was more discernible that morning. My husband left for work more encouraged, with an expectant heart on the upcoming events God had clearly shown us for his future.

Two months quickly passed, and then one day I got the call!

I was driving home from a day of shopping and took his call on my Bluetooth.

He informed me one of his former bosses had approached him, asking if he would be interested in a position they had created. It was right up his alley.

Suddenly, I was overcome by God's presence and had to pull my car to the side of the road. Barely able to contain myself, I said, "THIS IS IT! This is what God was speaking about in the prophecy!"

He said, "Well, we'll have to see."

I said, while tingling from head to toe with God's presence, "I KNOW this is it, and you HAVE the position!"

He let me know there was an interview process. Again, he stated he would have to wait and see. I chuckled silently, smiling, still covered in the Holy Ghost Goosebumps.

Another month passed, and the call from my husband finally came.

You know, the call informing me the prophetic word had entered his world.

Yes, he would be moving into the position Jesus had held for him at his company, and he was thrilled. Me? I knew it all along!

Eager to begin, he was once again amazed at the accuracy of God's intentions unfolding before him. He carried more confidence in his new role; in his usual way with excellence, he gave himself entirely to his new position.

This God-appointed position has opened doors, which were shut and has brought forth new levels of innovation and inspiration for my husband and his peers.

As I mentioned earlier, my husband was pondering retiring, but God had a *far more significant* plan. As you read on, you will see the power of the prophetic life and God's amazing grace.

Jeremiah 29:11(NIV): "For I know the plans I have for you,' declares the Lord, 'plans to prosper you and not to harm you, plans to give you hope and a future."

Hebrews 11:1 (NIV): "Now faith is confidence in what we hope for and assurance about what we do not see."

Romans 4:20 (NIV): "Yet Abraham did not waver through unbelief regarding the promise of God, but was strengthened in his faith, and gave glory to God."

"Lord, I pray that you find us trusting you, hoping for the best, and believing for the best. May we look forward to our future with expectation, anticipating You will show up and be all we need.

You let us know, in Your word, a future lays waiting for us, with plans to prosper us and not to harm us. I ask that when You see us sometimes fumbling along in our faith, You'll smile, letting us know You notice we've given what we know how to give and released to You our lives the only way we can." Amen.

Chapter 15

Who Opened the Door
– Fear Or Faith?

Throughout the last 34 years, with Jesus at the helm, my passionate desire has been to fall deeper in love with Him.

I've learned that trusting in myself is futile, but trusting with complete surrender to His will, is a place of rest, freeing me from trying to perform.

Being fully immersed in His plans is pleasing to Him, for His word lets me know it is impossible to please Him *without* faith. This is all I have ever longed for.

Hebrews 11:6 (NIV): "And without faith, it is impossible to please God because anyone who comes to Him must believe that He exists and that He rewards those who earnestly seek him."

One massive test of faith came to my husband and me in October 2017.

At that time, Steve was walking in his prophetic word, and God was using him dynamically.

He went in for a routine physical, which included a blood draw. His physician called the next day and let him know he needed to see him immediately.

The doctor told him the blood work revealed an extremely high PSA (prostate-specific antigen) count. The doctor recommended a biopsy and a C.T. scan to check for cancer. If a man has a PSA level above 4.0 or more, he is urged to have both procedures, and my husband had a PSA of 20.

We let the doctor know we were believers and would be praying about how to proceed; we decided to hold off and get more opinions before doing a biopsy.

Each time he went to see a doctor, I would have him call me from the doctor's office so that we could pray while the doctor was present. I genuinely believe that when we cover ourselves through an agreement in prayer, the enemy is blocked.

I informed the doctor, while on the phone, we believed in the power of prayer, and we knew God to be a miracle worker. I prayed a spirit-led prayer, thanked him for his time, and hung up the phone.

More opinions were gathered, and blood workups were conducted, but the news we had hoped for was not readily apparent.

In fact, my husband's PSA count was rapidly climbing.

Up to then, life in our home had been about overcoming the odds stacked against us and subsequently watching the Lord bring us through each fiery trial.

Steve and I had a foundation of God's Word laid; enabling us to stand on all God had done throughout our years together.

All of our victories were tucked away in our hearts. They were memorials placed like a red carpet before us, giving us a sturdy place to walk through any storm.

Every trial we had encountered and overcome, monuments were built within us both, written on the tablets of our hearts'.

What would we do with this news from the doctor, and who would answer our heart's door; fear or faith?

If fear answered the door, we would feel as if we were punched in the gut, with no ability to breathe. We knew fear would knock us back on our heels, allowing us to neither sleep nor eat.

Conversely, if faith answered the door, we would feel God's assurance and rest in our confidence in Jesus.

A faith-filled response has always shown us where we've placed our trust. Trust and hope are what sustain us where fear has no foundation, and peace anchors our souls.

Because Jesus is the Good News, and this news was not good, we prepared ourselves, *through faith*, to stand on the solid rock of Jesus as this storm blew past us!

God spoke in his word; He will keep us in perfect peace when our minds stayed on Him. He didn't say we would have partial peace; He made sure to use the word perfect!

Hebrews 4:12 (KJV): "For the word of God is quick, and powerful, and sharper than any two-edged sword, piercing even to the dividing asunder of soul and spirit, and of the joints and marrow, and is a discerner of the thoughts and intents of the heart."

Isaiah 26:3 (NLT): "You will keep in PERFECT peace all who trust in you, all whose thoughts are fixed on you."

Colossians 3:2 (NIV): "Set your minds on things above, not on earthly things."

"Lord, we know ALL things come by You or through You. We see the countless times when You have ushered in life, when death has come near, and You have brought to us a steady diet of Your Word, to sustain us when we feel weary or alone.

We cannot run from You, for You are stuck like glue to Your children. Lord, knowing You have provided all that is needed for our journey on this earth imparts great peace.

We are confident You who began a good work in us will bring it to completion, and we are to be as a pen in Your Hand as You write our stories daily.

We submit to You, Jesus, the Author and Finisher of our days. Our surrendering to You brings You such joy, and it brings us peace to know that our story ends well." Amen.

Chapter 16

Operating in Faith

We prayed and let only a handful of people know about the diagnosis. In the past, we had seen how fear and concern from well-meaning family and friends could impact us when we were standing on God's Word.

There is an old saying: "Bad news travels fast." We didn't view this as bad news; no, we considered it news, and God was letting us know how to pray.

We wanted to protect ourselves from words that would possibly be spoken from a place of fear, not faith. There is power when prayers are in agreement, coupled with faith.

Matthew 18:19 (NIV): "Again, truly I tell you that if two of you on earth agree about anything they ask for, it will be done for them by my Father in heaven."

We traveled out of state to a healing conference in February 2018. We continued to believe in a miracle, for both my husband as well as me.

I was having severe issues with my back; therefore, the doctor suggested I have more tests, which would eventually lead to surgery. We arrived at our hotel, threw our luggage in our room, and dashed off to the healing conference.

The meeting was unlike anything we had attended before.

During worship, it felt as though we were the choir of angels, and heaven DID come down and kiss us.

The wondrously glorious presence of God was genuine and palpable. After our praise and worship, testimonies were shared, which was refreshingly unique.

Whether people were sharing in person or on the humungous screen, the testimonies ignited faith. The atmosphere was charged with expectancy.

Nothing builds faith like hearing folks share stories of overcoming odds and having the impossible made possible.

Many people around us and in the arena were healed, including me. The next day, we attended the healing rooms and were touched even more.

The following day, we made our way back home, rejoicing and believing we both were healed, even though my husband did not feel tangibly touched as I had been.

When we returned, my husband decided to have a biopsy.

The results showed cancer had spread. The doctor let him know there was no treatment option; he was going to die. Again, we knew we had to be firm in our stand, keeping the door of faith open wide and the entrance to fear sealed SHUT!

During this time, my husband was also receiving ministry from some folks who use a format called "Restoring the Foundations."

It was perfect timing. All along our way, the Lord used these folks to pray over my husband, removing generational curses and more.

His father had died of prostate cancer years earlier, and we knew it was trying to take my husband's life too.

In April 2018, during an appointment, my husband's physician shared his shock and disbelief while reading the recent PSA report.

"Your PSA is 0.02!" He added, "I've never seen anything like it. It dropped from 54 to 0.02."

My hubby jumped up and said, Praise God, I am healed!"

The next PSA test showed the level was 0.00. The Dr said, "Your PSA is so low I cannot get a reading on it." Can we all just say, "PRAISE JESUS, He IS KING!"

To this day, my husband is healed, and we both continue to grow in faith.

Luke 1:37 (NLT): "For nothing is impossible with God."

Matthew 19:26 (NIV): "Jesus looked at them and said, 'With man this is impossible, but with God all things are possible.'"

Mark 9:23 (NIV): "'If you can?' said Jesus. 'Everything is possible for one who believes.'"

Revelation 12:11 (KJV): "And they overcome him (satan), by the blood of the Lamb, and by the word of their testimony; and they loved not their lives unto death."

"Lord, we are thankful, grateful, and filled with even more expectations of all that is in store for our lives.

You crushed the enemy before we were even born, and You will continue being the Dominator over satan's schemes.

Thank You for letting us know, before we engaged in battle with the enemy, that we WIN! Beginning our day with confidence, knowing You have our backs, imparts courage to face the giants we may encounter.

Whether it's someone who is rude or angry, someone who is in our face, or a diagnosis with a grim ending, You'll consistently bring about GOOD! Submitting to our GOOD Father is not hard to accomplish, Lord. Therefore, we will be the branch resting in You, our Vine." Amen.

Chapter 17

The Kingdom of God Is Ours!

Throughout my 35 years of walking with Jesus, I have learned that it *does* matter who I believe and where I place my trust.

My husband and I are not against doctors; however, we believe in allowing God to have His final say in our lives.

We try and not allow a physician's terminal prognosis be the final authoritative word.

I remember a pastor said, "The moment a crisis becomes bigger than my own awareness of God, I will live in reaction to the problem. If I live in reaction to the problem, the devil will have influence in setting my agenda."

As I have shared throughout my book, I must be pro-active in taking my thoughts captive, not giving the devil access to my mind. I must disregard the fear-filled rhetoric the enemy spews forth in an attempt to gain access to my mental activity, and replace it with God's word.

My mind is an active place, and if I allow my thoughts to run wild, they will eventually lead me down a dark path of hopelessness.

The enemy intends to significantly impact my actions, through his intimidation, and I must stop the dialogue, assaulting my thoughts.

If fear influences my speculations on life, I must exercise my faith, pushing back the world of demonic terror, trying to control me.

If faith connects me to God's kingdom power, what does fear connect me to?

When fear and anxiety are trying to control me, I will react in my emotions and *not* have the ability to hear the Holy Spirit; nor respond to Jesus.

Daily, I seek to attain God's supernatural ability and Kingdom power, working through me as I relinquish my life into His hands.

Matthew 12:28 (NIV): "But if it is by the Spirit of God that I drive out demons, then the kingdom of God has come upon you."

The Greek meaning of "kingdom" is the foundation of power, rule, realm, and reigning. The word "reign," in the Greek, means to exercise authority.

God gave me authority over the enemy, and fear is not our friend—it is our adversary.

Fear is continually working against God's will for me, exerting its bold mission to destroy my life.

Faith continually stands behind, before, and on either side of me. Hope and faith will usher me into my destiny, and my inheritance, to live in my Promised Land.

Ephesians 3:20 (NIV): "Now to Him who is able to do immeasurably more than all we ask or imagine, according to his power that is at work within us."

I know there are giants in my promised land and one way of destroying them is to *not* be frightened or intimidated by them.

Fear screams at the top of its lungs, "Hang on for your life, and never let go!" Faith whispers, "Let go and take My hand. I will lead you to My quiet place, hiding safely beneath My peace."

Job 3:25 (KJV): "For the thing which I greatly fear is come upon me and that which I was afraid of is come unto me."

This is an authoritative scripture. God shows us that fear can attract the realm of darkness, and the very thing we fear will end up at our doorstep.

Matthew 6:33 (NIV): "But seek first his kingdom and his righteousness, and all these things will be given to you as well."

God is longing for us to exercise our God-given authority and dominion; reigning in his glorious power, overcoming all obstacles, and accessing His realm of authority.

Faith is waiting to meet us face to face, and His name is Jesus!

Mark 16:17 (NIV): "And these signs will accompany these who believe: In My name they will drive out demons; they will speak in new tongues; they will pick up snakes with their hands; and when they drink deadly poison, it will not hurt them at all; they will place their hands on sick people, and they will get well."

Matthew 16:24 (NIV): "Then Jesus said to his disciples, 'Whoever wants to be my disciple must deny themselves and take up their cross and follow me.'"

"Lord Jesus, we want to be children of God, who look behind and see that we have lived a life of believing, with miracles following!

We've consistently longed to lay our hearts and trust at the feet of You, Jesus, and be taken into Your Holy place; having tangible impartations of Your love and power.

May our testimonies create a fierce wall of protection against the assaults of the enemy.

May we run to You, Lord, and not to the phone to call a friend. I pray that we understand the only help that lasts is coming to You, our Helper and Comforter, Who longs to rescue us all day long.

Forgive us, Lord, for not allowing You to take us before mountains You are able to move. May we clearly see You from the spirit of God dwelling within, and not from our hearts, which can deceive us."
Amen.

Chapter 18

Facing Giants, Winning Battles

The Lord has directed me to either stand, fly out of state, or go by boat into frightful looking situations and pray.

Not long ago, I walked into a local store, and a huge man was there, yelling VERY loud and causing people to back away in fear.

I immediately grabbed my cart and walked to the back of the store, and began shopping.

I remember thinking, 'He will be gone by the time I am done.' I made my way through the store, gathering the items on my list, and then moved toward the registers.

Much to my dismay, the man's screaming continued, and the line he was in was not moving.

I went to the register as far from him as possible and waited, hoping to depart quickly.

The Lord spoke to my heart: "Why are you in fear? I want you to stand behind him and pray, binding the enemy who is controlling him, trying to rattle and intimidate others."

Wanting to respond to the Lord quickly, I moved behind the man and began praying. Within seconds, he quieted down, and the line began to quickly move and he left the store.

Another time, I was visiting a friend at her home, and while I was there, she gave me a tour.

We went outside to her backyard. As soon as we stepped out, two enormous Doberman Pinschers came running up to my friend's chain link fence.

THANKFULLY, there WAS a fence, as had there not been one, we most likely would have been fleeing for our lives.

The Spirit of God rose within me and went toward the fence. I pointed my finger, and with a bold and thunderous voice, I began rebuking the spirit of fear.

Right before our eyes, the dogs began to yelp while backing away from the fence.

It was quite a sight to see! I love watching God show up and show off His power.

I've had cars following too close, when driving, and when I ask the angels to push them off my bumper—bam, done!

It has taken time for me to understand I'm not of this world; I am in it.

God lets me know I am not here for me, I am here for Him, and He has equipped me to win every battle!

When I quickly identify the spirits coming AT me, I step into my spirit man and deflect the assaults with my Shield of Faith.

Putting on the Armor of God is much like a superhero jumping into his suit being transformed into a powerful weapon to destroy the evil forces.

I love watching God show up and display His power when I am walking in His Kingdom realm on earth.

God's perfect love casts out fear, and I want to be filled to the brim with His love.

Ephesians 6:11 (NIV): "Put on the whole armor of God so that you can take your stand against the devil's schemes."

Ephesians 6:12 (NIV): "For our struggle is not against flesh and blood, but against the rulers, against the authorities, against the powers of this dark world and against spiritual forces of evil in the heavenly realm."

Ephesians 3:17 (NIV): "So that you, being rooted and grounded and established in love."

Greek: Rooted—firmly established. Grounded—having a firm foundation.

1 John 4:18 (NIV): "There is NO fear in love. But perfect love drives OUT fear; because fear has to do with punishment. The one who fears is not made perfect in love."

"Lord, may we be swept up in Your love, taken into Your sanctuary, where we are placed in Your unfailing rest.

May we daily be captured by Your peace, cradled by Your flawless Word, and held in unbroken unity. Let us smell the scent of heaven's aroma penetrating our soul.

Pull us in, arrest our hearts, sit us down, and make us one. There will never be anyone greater than You, Lord. Therefore, yielding our lives ushers in indescribable trust. Subdue us with Your strong arm if You catch a glimpse of us wandering far off and alone.

Your strength brings comfort, while angelic songs take flight as we listen to sounds being strummed on heaven's floor. We'll step away from fear's luring snare, which once persuaded.

The temptations enticing us into fear's dark world cannot take us prisoner, nor interrupt one moment with You.

There will be no trace of piercing darkness, but only Your great grace drawing us away, closing doors to the uncertainty we feel.

Gates will swing open; exit signs will shine through confusion, pointing the way to our escape.

You are our Hope and Shield, and a place of rest in the midst of storms. You ARE our passage out. Whether it is out of fear, discouragement, or hopelessness, You make a way, leading straight to YOU!" Amen.

Chapter 19

Our Ministry Boats

Our love for boats and people has kept us on the water for over 20 years. We believe God gives us the desires of our hearts, and we feel blessed to be able to continue our boat ministry here in our home state.

We purchased a boat after our first year of living back here. This vessel was a beauty, but after the first year and a half, it became apparent this boat would not be the one we would continue with.

We had bitten off more than we could chew if you will, and this boat was far too big for us to navigate on our own.

After putting it up for sale, we got an offer fairly quickly. We had not found another boat, and my husband said, "If we sell her and don't have another boat, we may miss out on being on the water this summer."

I chuckled because isn't that typically how things go? Sell one, before you find another?

It was not what God had told us in previous years if you remember our story.

God had told my husband when trying to sell our boat after our move, "Buy a boat here, and the other one will sell."

Now it was: "Sell a boat and trust God to provide another one in time for the summer boating season."

Our friend and boat salesman kept in close contact with us, letting us know he could not find a thing.

While we were finishing the sale of our boat, my husband was on the Web, doing his usual search for boats. He said, "Have you seen this one, honey?"

I had not; therefore, we made plans to attend the boat show, where the boat was located the following day.

After arriving and going on board, we fell in love immediately.

There were two other couples on board who loved this vessel as well, and at first, I was a little nervous, questioning if this was "The one."

She was a used boat, which we always sought out, but this one had been kept up and looked new.

We made an offer right away, and the boat ended up becoming ours.

I don't know why I am amazed when things fall quickly into place, because it has always been an indicator God is at work!

There was—and has been—ease when we have allowed God to lead in our lives.

We have found the Lord wants us to discover more of Him; He likes to play hide-n-seek. He desires that we pursue Him because the things hidden from us will be revealed and when it is, it is like finding gold.

After hearing from the Lord, we experience difficulties, we stop and ask, "Lord, did we move ahead of You, or did You open the door or us?"

Sometimes there is opposition, and it is something to pray through, as it feels like warfare in the spirit realm.

Other times, we consistently ask questions as we move toward what we have asked the Lord for.

This boat was everything we had prayed for and more. We've taken many folks out to pray, watch the whales, kayak, or just sit and enjoy the weather.

We have auctioned off boat trips at our daughter's school, and other fundraisers; as we love taking folks out whom we've never met; it means we get to share Jesus.

At times, we are giddy as we share our love for the Lord, and the many testimonies, which is our main reason for inviting folks out

Matthew 6:33 (GW): "But first, be concerned about His Kingdom and what has His approval. Then all these things will be provided for you."

Matthew 7:7 (NIV): "Ask and it will be given; seek and you will find; knock and the door will be opened to you."

Psalm 37:4-5 (NIV): "Take delight in the Lord, and he will give you the desires of your heart. Commit your way to the Lord; trust in him and He will do this: He will make your righteous reward shine like the dawn, your justice like the noonday sun."

Isaiah 22:22 (NIV): "I will place on his shoulder the key to the house of David; what he opens no one can shut, and what he shuts no one can open."

"Lord Jesus, we dedicate our lives to you each and every day.

Moment by moment we release our plans into Your loving hands, as we know Your hands open and close doors.

What You have given to us, the very breath we breathe, is counted a blessing.

Let us take what has been given and use it for Your glory, and not our own.

May the praises of our lips, and the grateful hearts we carry within, be pleasing to You, Lord.

Thanksgiving and praise, honor and glory, belong to You, Lord Jesus our King.

Let us hold fast to the hem of Your garment, for within, it holds power to release us into our destiny."
Amen.

Chapter 20

Falling in Love
With My King

Years ago, a couple of months after we moved into our home, I met a woman who lived next door.

Wanting to get acquainted, we got together for a visit. Friends who know me well would say I am forthcoming about my love for Jesus, and in keeping with tradition, I let her know I was a Christian right away.

To be honest, I have a hard time not talking about the love of my life: Jesus!

After I shared my affection for the Lord, she began telling me about ALL she had done. "I was a chaplain at Providence Hospital, I taught Sunday school at my church for years, I left the country on mission trips," she declared.

On and on, she told me about ALL she had done. I listened politely, and when it was my time to speak, I shared my enormous list of miracles, and ALL God had done.

After she left, God immediately and tenderly spoke: "Sherrie, did you notice? She told you about all she had done, and you shared ALL I have done! You pointed to Me while she pointed to herself."

Friends, I am *not* a religious person, I am in a relationship, surrendered to a POWER-filled God.

Jesus has Healed, Delivered, and Provided for me. He is my Savior, Restorer of all I had lost, and so much more. God longs to BE all any of us will ever need.

I have nothing to offer of my own, but I am joined to my Father, Who lets me know *greater things* than He did, will I be equipped to do.

There is, however, a requirement, which is: that I *believe*.

I pray the faith-filled stories and testimonies I've shared will compel you to launch out and allow God to place you in front of impossibilities. In my 35 years of serving the Lord, I have *never* seen Jesus NOT do the impossible for me because it is certainly possible for Him; He is God.

Time and again, I stand back and watch while Jesus sweetly and tenderly loves me through some otherwise turbulent times.

Mark 9:23 (NIV): "All things are possible if you only believe."

Philippians 4:19 (NIV): "And my God will meet all your needs according to the riches of His glory in Christ Jesus."

Deuteronomy 10:21 (NIV): "He is the one you praise; he is your God, who performed for you those great and awesome wonders you saw with your own eyes."

"Lord Jesus, we look to You, for You alone hold the stars in their place, and unveil the sun. You've placed the earth beneath as Your footstool and filled the land with the seas.

You wrote out the plans for our lives, before the foundation of the universe was laid.

Mighty God, You hold all our days and nights, and sustain our bodies with Your great Grace and Love.

We look to You for all that pertains to our lives and we welcome Your plans, laying aside our own. Forgive us for trusting ourselves, making arrangements that don't include You.

If we feel anxious, remind us, Lord, You have pulled us into the cleft of Your Rock and hidden us away from the tear-filled days, cloaking our view of Your sustaining power.

We can unceasingly trust You, for You tug on the sun and stars, bringing in light and ushering in the quiet rest the darkness provides.

As we sink back into Your security, we exhale, releasing our Will and granting access to usher in Yours.

If we feel feeble in our ability, You whisper, 'I am your strength,' and if we question our existence, You announce, 'I created you to thrive and burst forth with the love I've generously imparted.'

We offer ourselves to our Savior, for You, Lord, preserve our days, buoying us if we feel we're sinking in the troublesome sands of adversity.

We celebrate and embrace each moment of our day, for without You we would not have one." Amen.

Chapter 21

Living in Gratitude

I believe when we walk in generosity, lavishing God with our love and adoration, we draw His attention and favor into our lives!

We must *not* feel guilty about expecting God to open doors of favor for us. His word promises Grace and abundance before Him and before man.

When we let Him know all we have is His, there isn't anything He won't give us.

A few years ago, I had a vivid dream. A woman prayed, asking for her house sell.

Jesus heard her request and walked toward God, like in a courtroom. He said to Father God, "Your daughter asked for her house to sell, may I grant her petition?" Before God could answer, Jesus turned to hear her answer the phone.

He heard her say to her friend, "No, this house is never going to sell.

The stairs are killing my knees, I'm sick and tired of yard work, and my husband is driving me crazy!" Jesus turned back to Father God and said, "Never mind, she changed her mind.

I guess she doesn't remember this is the house she asked for in prayer. She used to love the stairs and yard work, and she used to adore her husband."

Friends, I ask the Lord to daily show me if I am praying one thing and speaking words of unbelief soon after.

I regularly ask Jesus to forgive me for anything I've spoken, opposing His Kingdom and ask Him to destroy any strongholds or fortresses' my negative chatter, may have built.

James 1:8 (NIV): "He is a double-minded man, unstable in ALL his ways." Philippians 2:2 (NIV): "Fulfill my joy by being like-minded, having the same love, being of one mind."

Folks, it matters what we believe, Who we believe and what we say.

I also know the way out of frustration and grumbling, is by being grateful and thankful.

My words are powerful; whether they are grumbling or thanking, they have the power to bless or curse.

If I ask the Lord for something in prayer, and then complain and grumble, my prayers will not be heard or fulfilled.

Am I listening to the news on television or social media, then throwing out my two-cents? If so, are my prayers pulling down the strongholds and arguments of the negative press?

Do I enter into unfruitful conversations having nothing to do with furthering God's plans?

If I pray one thing and say another, I'll create instability in my emotions, missing out on living in God's perfect peace.

Perhaps having grown up in a home with complaining and little gratitude made me more aware of the world of words around me.

I find it amazing that I see few expressions of gratitude.

Ever since I can remember, I have tried to be grateful and blessed to even be alive.

Ephesians 3:16-19 (NIV): "I pray that out of his glorious riches he may strengthen you with power through his Spirit in your inner being, so that Christ may dwell in your hearts through faith."

Isaiah 26:3 (NIV): "You'll keep him in perfect peace whose mind is stayed on You because he trusts You."

Psalms 51:10 (NIV): "Create in me a pure heart, O God, and renew a right spirit and mind within me."

Ephesians 3:16-19 (NIV): "I pray out of His glorious riches He may strengthen you with power through His Spirit in your inner being so that Christ may dwell in your hearts through faith. And I pray you, being rooted and established in love, may have power, together with all the Lord's holy people, to grasp how wide and long and high and deep is the love of Christ and to know this love that surpasses knowledge—that you may be filled to the measure of all the fullness of God."

Jesus may we all step away from any negative words we may think or say.

I pray we trust You to inscribe Your word on the tablets of our hearts and tongues. May our lips declare Your goodness, Your faithfulness and Righteousness.

As we are pulled into Your world, we will see You rescued us from ourselves and even our own negative words. Thank You for forgiving us Lord, over and over. Your mercies are new every morning, and we will choose to bathe ourselves in them. May You find us saturated in Your loving-kindness', buoyed in the sea of Your Love! Amen

Chapter 22

In Closing

Over 29 years ago, I faced one of the most significant challenges I had ever encountered. I was married when my husband left me to face over $200,000 in debt when I was four months pregnant.

The following years would prove to be the most exciting and supernatural times I have ever lived through. The Lord and His powerful provision delivered me out of ninety-nine percent of my debt.

As I prayed and reached out to Jesus as my Provider, Deliverer, Comforter, and Restorer of all I had lost, God supernaturally and divinely supplied all I needed.

It seems surreal now, but I was able to step into God's peace and literally watch Him dismantle all of the obstacles that lay before me.

I watched God *supernaturally* pay off the $200,000 debt I had incurred. I had *no* maternity on my Blue Cross insurance, and yet they paid for *everything*!

My ex-husband left me with $100,000 in debt in the form of state taxes. However, the Lord saw that I did not have to pay it back, which was what my attorney said would happen for sure.

On and on, the miracles kept coming.

Whatever challenges I have found and do find before me, He walks straight on in and over them, bringing me into my promises and answered prayers!

Friends, Jesus longs to be for us, all we need – now and forever.

Back then, I was thrown into trials I did not ask for.

For the last 23 years of my current marriage, we have gone before the Lord, letting Him know we are WILLING to be placed before impossibilities. He has, and we've watched them all bow to the Name of Jesus.

We used to try to take care of our needs—until our eyes were supernaturally opened. We *finally* understood that God wants to show up in His power and demonstrate through us, and to the world around us, just WHO HE IS!

He cannot display His power, if we are unwilling to be placed in front of mountains that cannot be moved, without a supernatural move of our King Jesus.

My hope is for you to feel infused with faith, and hope, compelling you to leave the safe harbor of reason and logic and step onto the waters of great grace and abundance in Jesus Christ!

My book is named Willingly, because it is who I've become; some who willingly walks with Jesus, letting Him take me places I would not normally be inclined to go.

About The Author

Sherrie Brown is the Bestselling Author of "Life Within His Promises."

She is also a Visioneer and Inventor, having attained two (2) U.S. Design Patents on Leg Wear, and is the owner of Classy Calves™ She is also owned and operated a Hair Salon for 24 years.

She is a wife, mother and an-up-and coming speaker, who loves to spend time on her family's boat, in the vast waters of the Puget Sound.

Sherrie's greatest joy is ministering to believers who struggle to hear from Jesus or have an encounter with Him. God has given her wisdom and skill through the Holy Spirit to usher healing into the lives of believers who've not known how to access their God-given authority and power. Sherrie takes God's beloved children on a healing journey, bringing them into their Promise Land filled with faith and hope.

Please Rate My Book

I'd be honored if you would take a few moments to rate this book on Amazon.com.

A five-star rating and a short comment ("Inspiring," or "Excellent and empowering!") would be much appreciated. Longer, positive comments are great as well.

If you feel like this book should be rated at three stars or fewer, please hold off posting your thoughts on Amazon.

Instead, please send your feedback directly to me so that I can use it to improve the next edition. I'm committed to providing the best value to my customers and readers, and your thoughts can make that possible.

You may reach me at:
ClassyCalves@gmail.com.

With gratitude,

Sherrie Brown

Made in the USA
Coppell, TX
09 November 2020

41039462R00163